Property of

W9-BJD-996
LIBRARY

The New Age
MASQUERADE

Family of Faith Library

The New Age
MASQUERADE

The Hidden Agenda in Your Child's Classroom

Eric Buehrer

Wolgemuth & Hyatt, Publishers, Inc.
Brentwood, Tennessee

The mission of Wolgemuth & Hyatt, Publishers, Inc. is to publish and distribute books that lead individuals toward:

- A personal faith in the one true God: Father, Son, and Holy Spirit;

- A lifestyle of practical discipleship; and

- A worldview that is consistent with the historic, Christian faith.

Moreover, the Company endeavors to accomplish this mission at a reasonable profit and in a manner which glorifies God and serves His Kingdom.

© 1990 by Eric Buehrer. All rights reserved.
Published September 1990. First Edition.
Printed in the United States of America.
97 96 95 94 93 92 91 90   8 7 6 5 4 3 2 (Second Printing, November 1990)

No part of this publication may be reproduced, stored in a retrieval system, or transmitted in any form by any means, electronic, mechanical, photocopy, recording, or otherwise, without the prior written permission of the publisher, except for brief quotations in critical reviews or articles.

Unless otherwise noted, all Scripture quotations are from the New King James Version of the Bible, © 1979, 1980, 1982, 1984 by Thomas Nelson, Inc., Nashville, Tennessee and are used by permission.

Wolgemuth & Hyatt, Publishers, Inc.
1749 Mallory Lane, Suite 110
Brentwood, Tennessee 37027

Library of Congress Cataloging-in-Publication Data

Buehrer, Eric.
    The New Age masquerade : the hidden agenda in your child's classroom / Eric Buehrer.
        p.   cm.
    Includes bibliographical references.
    ISBN 1-56121-019-6
    1. Religion in the public schools—United States—Case studies.
2. New Age movement—United States—Case studies. 3. Public schools—United States—Case studies. 4. New Age movement—Controversial literature. I. Title.
LC111.B78 1990
370.11—dc20

                                                                    90-40085
                                                                        CIP

To my parents, Paul and Marilyn,
for teaching me how to think
and encouraging me
to pursue my dreams.

CONTENTS

ACKNOWLEDGMENTS

A number of people helped me along the way, and without them I wouldn't have written this book. I'd like to thank John Wilson for getting me started; Chris Shardelman for providing me with volumes of documents; Dr. Robert Simonds for reminding me that the book should be completed within our lifetime; Tom Tancredo and Greg Cunningham for letting me know I wasn't alone; and the hundreds of parents and teachers whose questions have spurred me on to find answers.

PART ONE

CLASSROOM MASQUERADE

TURNING THE HEARTS OF THE YOUNG

*Any revolutionary change must be preceded by
a passive, affirmative, non-challenging attitude
toward change among the masses of our people.*

Saul Alinsky

I picked up the telephone in my office at the national headquarters of Citizens for Excellence in Education. On the other end of the line was the emotion-filled voice of a woman. "I teach in the Milwaukee area, and I am forced every week to allow a guidance counselor to lead my third-grade class through a meditation exercise while they sit cross-legged on the floor." The teacher went on to explain, "This counselor teaches the children to use a secret word in a chant in order to achieve what she calls *sparkle mind*. She then tells the children to visualize a dragon named Ponsje walking toward them. This dragon, the counselor says, is your personal friend who will help you whenever you have a problem." The Christian teacher was frustrated and a problem." The Christian teacher was frustrated and wanted to know what she could do to stop this New Age mystic ritual.

My telephone rang again. This time a mother from Nebraska told me of a program in her son's school that has the children using guided imagery, visualization, and meditation. The teacher's manual says to have the children touch a magic wand or ring to help them meditate. She is concerned about a warning the authors of the program issue stating that students may experience nausea, tightness of the chest, pulse increase, shaky limbs, and sweats.

"What do I do?" she asked.

In a seemingly unrelated incident, a proposed social studies program for New York schools declares that all minorities have been "victims of an intellectual and educational oppression that has characterized the culture and institutions of the United States and the European world for centuries." The program's cure? Radical elimination of teaching about Western civilization in public schools.

A program for first graders in Washington state instructs children that their faith is not true but only an indoctrination of Western values.

A teacher-trainer's textbook helped me see the relationship between leading children in Nebraska through meditation exercises and New York's call for the overthrow of Western cultural values. The textbook for teachers asserts that Americans may seek to cling to the language of old, secular creeds like those of Western civilization, and they may strongly desire to hold on to "old" religions. But unless a new faith "overcomes the old ideologies and creates planetary synthesis, world government is doomed."

New Age meditation in the classroom? One world government taught as the goal for public school teachers? My brain had had enough for one day. That night, as I lay in bed, I drifted off to sleep and had a dream . . .

🙚 🙚 🙚

The class of fresh fourth graders wiggled excitedly in their desk chairs awaiting Ms. Johnson to put down her pen, look up from her note pad, and begin the first day of school.

Ms. Johnson stood up as the bell rang to begin the morning.

"Welcome to planet Earth," she said with a warm smile. The children looked puzzled. Other teachers had started with "Welcome to the third grade" or "Welcome to my classroom," but never this.

"Isn't it a wonderful day today?" she continued. The children nodded in eager agreement. "Did you know that children just like yourselves are starting school all over the world today?"

Ms. Johnson asked a red-headed boy on the front row if he would get the globe from the shelf and bring it to her. Slowly she rotated the globe of Earth and talked about the millions of children all starting school.

"And do you know how many are fourth graders?" she asked. "Millions!" she whispered with excitement. The entire class had their eyes fixed on Ms. Johnson and her globe.

Johnny thought to himself about the millions of fourth graders around the world as he watched the globe rotate. He remembered seeing a TV show about children in Japan.

"Where's Japan?" he asked.

"That is a very good question," the teacher replied. "It is always good to find countries on the globe." She rotated the globe until Japan faced the class. "Here it is," she said, delicately pointing to the island country.

"Can anyone show us where we are?" Hands shot into the air.

Sally was chosen, and she proudly marched to the front of the classroom and pointed to the United States.

"Very good," said Ms. Johnson. The teacher continued for a while longer showing the children where America is in relation to the rest of the world's fourth graders.

"What do we do at the beginning of every school day?" Ms. Johnson asked.

"We say the Pledge," Judy spoke up.

"That's right," said the teacher. "What does a pledge mean?"

The children looked puzzled for a moment. Then Johnny raised his hand.

"It means you're gonna do what you say you're gonna do," he volunteered.

"That's an excellent answer." Ms. Johnson was very pleased. "So a pledge is a promise. And when we say the Pledge we are promising good things."

The children nodded in agreement. Sally remembered how her father had once said the Pledge was a good thing to do.

Ms. Johnson went on, "Now our country is run by many good people who have promised to do good things for us. Since they already have pledged to help our country, who can we pledge to help?"

The children thought for a moment. Kathy raised her hand. "Each other?" she said with a hesitation.

"That is an excellent idea," the teacher replied. "Helping other fourth graders is a wonderful idea!"

The class smiled in unison. They liked Ms. Johnson. She was kind, and the way she said things made the children feel warm inside.

"What if we promised to help all the fourth graders in the world?"

"In the whole world?" Jimmy blurted out. "How can we do that?" he asked in disbelief.

"That is a very good question, Jimmy," she replied. "Of course, just the few of us can't help *all* the fourth graders in the world. But it wouldn't be nice just to promise good things to only us."

That seemed fair, and Jimmy relaxed in his chair.

"If you could promise *anything* to your fourth-grade classmates around the world, what would it be?" the teacher asked.

"Easy homework assignments," someone said.

The class laughed and so did Ms. Johnson.

"How about some other things?" she asked.

"Fun," said Sally.

Ms. Johnson wrote the word *Fun* on the chalkboard.

Johnny raised his hand, "I wish those kids in Africa could have some food."

Ms. Johnson wrote *Food* on the board.

"How about no war," offered Jimmy.

"That is a good one," Ms. Johnson said as she wrote it on the board.

"How 'bout no pollution?" offered one girl.

Ms. Johnson wrote the words *a clean environment* on the board.

"So now let's say our own pledge to our classmates around the world," she said.

All the children stood up. They liked the idea of doing something different. In their second- and third-grade classes they always said the same old thing. It would be fun to try something new.

"Let's put our hand over our heart and recite our new pledge to our classmates around the world," she directed.

All the children began in unison: "I pledge allegiance to the flag of the . . . "

"Wait!" Ms. Johnson stopped the class. "If we are going to wish good things to the fourth graders of the world, we need to have a flag for all of them, not just *our* country."

"How do we do that?" asked Billy. "There are too many countries."

Ms. Johnson went to the storage closet and pulled out a pretty blue satin flag with an emblem of the world on it.

"This," she explained with a smile, "is a flag that represents all the countries of the world. It was designed by all the nations of the earth and represents the United Nations."

She asked a boy to stand on a chair and replace the old flag with the new one.

"We'll keep our old flag here in the storage closet. It is always good to be proud of our country, just like we are proud of our school. We'll use it on very special days."

She wrote on the chalkboard the words to the new pledge.

"Now, let's continue with our pledge," she said.

The children put their hands over their hearts and began again: "I pledge allegiance to the flag of the United Nations and to all the fourth graders it represents. I wish them fun, enough food to eat, no war, and a clean environment, a world with liberty and justice for all."

The class sat down.

"It is good to pledge to having no war," Ms. Johnson explained. "That is something we must always remember. How many of you are worried about nuclear war?"

Every one of the children raised their hands. "Someday we may have a nuclear war," she continued more seriously.

Billy spoke up, "It sure seems funny that we all want peace, but our leaders keep preparing for war." Ms. Johnson smiled in agreement.

Sally interjected, "My dad says that we have peace *because* of our strong defense."

"Some people think that, Sally. But class, do you feel peaceful about nuclear war?" the teacher asked.

Everybody shook their heads.

"And anyway," she continued, "it certainly doesn't seem right to terrorize all the fourth graders in the world just so *we* can feel safe—and then we realize that *we* don't feel safe after all. It just doesn't make sense."

"Yeah," said Ruthie. "But what can we do?"

"Later on in the year we can write letters to our leaders and ask them to stop making bombs," Ms. Johnson said.

The children smiled with a sense of relief. Writing letters to the president sounded fun and important.

"My dad says that nuclear defense is important," Sally said again, this time a little less confidently.

Ms. Johnson folded her soft hands in front of her. "Some people think that way. And I understand it. For the last one hundred years we have had a lot of wars around the world. But we are only a few years away from a new century. In the twenty-first century, we are going to be beyond war.

"Your dad's way of thinking is right for him. But it may not be right for you when you are a grown-up."

Ms. Johnson pointed to a poster on the wall and asked the class to recite what it said.

"The only thing you can count on is change."

"Everything changes," she continued. "The way you think about things will be different from the way your parents think about things. Your values may not be their values."

"But my mom says that I need to listen to her about what is right and wrong," Billy said.

"That's right," said the teacher. "It is always good to listen to what others have to say. But what someone else thinks is right may not be right for you."

"For example," she continued, "your parents' parents—your grandparents—thought that no stores should be open on Sunday. Now all the stores are open on Sunday."

Johnny thought about his dad working in the mall each Sunday afternoon. "Yeah," he said. "My dad doesn't believe what his dad believed."

"You see," said Ms. Johnson, "everything changes. It's always good to listen to your parents because they are very wise people. But your way may be different from theirs. After all, you are going to be grown-ups in a brand-new century."

The children thought about that. They liked the idea of growing up in their own century. No one had ever pointed that out before. More and more the children found that they liked Ms. Johnson. She made them feel special.

"Well, my mom says the Bible doesn't change," said Kathy.

"Your mom is right," the teacher replied. "The Bible doesn't change. But there are lots of religions in the world, and a lot of people don't even know about the Bible. How do you know the Bible is right?" Ms. Johnson asked Kathy.

"I believe it is."

"That is a very good thing to do," said Ms. Johnson with a smile. "It is good to believe in something and to look to something for guidance. But do you *know* that you are right?"

"My Sunday school teacher says the Bible is the Word of God," said Kathy.

"But how do you *know* that?" questioned the teacher.

"I just believe it," said Kathy.

"That is right," Ms. Johnson said gently. "But there are many religions in the world, and they all believe that they are right. You wouldn't want to say that only you are right and everyone else in the entire world is wrong, would you?"

"Well . . . no," said Kathy.

Ms. Johnson reassured the child. "I think believing in something is good, Kathy. But remember that there are a lot of other ways to look at something. And you would be saying that you were God if you thought that *only* you were right."

Kathy looked bewildered. But it certainly seemed to make sense, and she didn't want to offend God by thinking that *she* knew everything. *After all,* she thought to herself, *if other people believed other things about the Bible, He probably worked it all out in Heaven anyway.*

She thought about her pastor each Sunday morning shouting about how you had to believe the Bible if you wanted to go to Heaven. *His ideas certainly didn't seem very nice,* she thought. *And anyway, his shouting always makes me feel bad.* Ms. Johnson made her feel good.

Ms. Johnson explained to the class that she wanted them to look on the globe or in an atlas and, working together, list as many countries in the world as they could find. The children scurried around the room in a buzz of activity.

As Ms. Johnson watched the classroom full of children, she thought about the past couple of years and how her program of global education had eventually been adopted by the school district. It hadn't been easy.

After she had attended the initial global education workshops sponsored by the state, she returned to the district to implement a pilot program. There were faculty committees and school board meetings in which she explained the program and garnered support. Of course, she couldn't expect everyone to fully appreciate the full extent to which the program would change children's values and attitudes for the better. That's why she had so cleverly talked only of the broad goals of increasing world awareness. *You can't appear too radical,* she reminded herself.

Gradually the rest of the district saw the need for "expanding the vision" of the staff.

She thought back on the parents who objected to the new programs. Those religious people—always thinking they are right, always wanting to censor any new ideas. She had never realized just how extensive a network the Radical Right had and how many white supremists were masquerading as evangelicals. Her teachers' union material had been right about that all along. Bigots! All of them. Ignorant bigots.

But she had won. *Parents always protest new things*, she reminded herself. *But they wear out.* After all, she is paid to work in the school. All these parents have other things to occupy their time. She remembered how the superintendent formed committees with an even number of opposition parents and her colleagues who agreed with her. That was a setback. She had wanted greater representation for the district's teachers. After all, they were going to have to teach the program; they were professionals. She chuckled to herself as she remembered how she made a brilliant move when she scheduled the meetings on Wednesday night. Perfect! Those dumb Christians. They would never dream of missing one of their prayer meetings. Wouldn't want to lose points in Heaven. So they rarely showed up at the global education committee meetings. She got everything she wanted. Oh, she had thrown them a few bones. The section on meditation and contacting a personal spirit guide was removed, but it would be easy to reinstate that next year with a new label: thinking skills.

Parents always fade away, she thought to herself. *We can outlast them every time.*

Of course, she was grateful to the local news media. She really couldn't have done it without them. All those stories about world pollution, trade problems, terrorism, and population explosion were broadcast just at the right time. And when those fundamentalists came out of the woodwork, the media really did a job on them.

Some teachers didn't really like the new program either. They thought it was too political and "just plain weird," she recalled old Lester McNabb saying. But that was to be expected. When the superintendent offered them early retirement, a lot of them took it. Those that didn't . . . *well, this year we have them going to twice as many in-service, re-education classes. And if that doesn't work, there are other ways to push them out. They are the old guard, anyway. We need more fresh blood,* she thought to herself.

"Look, Ms. Johnson. Look what I found," Jimmy said holding up a clipping from National Geographic magazine. He held up a picture of a Hindu guru in a deep trance while sitting in the lotus position. "What's that man doing?" he asked.

"Oh," said Ms. Johnson, "he's learning to think better while talking to his special spirit guide. That's something we will be doing a lot of later on this year."

"All right!" said the boy with excitement as he ran back to the group he was working with. "This is going to be a fun year!"

The teacher looked across the classroom full of children intently working on their global assignment and thought about the children from kindergarten through twelfth grade throughout the district all going through the new program. She felt a warmth well up in her chest as she pondered her contribution toward the new age of global government.

ਣ ਣ ਣ

I awoke from my dream. That day at my office, I read a quote from a leading professor of education, Philip Vander Velde, in his textbook for public school teachers, *Global Mandate*. "[A] new world order is necessary if we are to live in harmony with each other. . . . The task of re-ordering our traditional values and institutions should be one of the major objectives of our schools."[1]

I pinched myself. Was I still dreaming?

2

MASKED VISION

Social engineering is the creation of millenarian intellectuals who believe they can refashion the universe by the light of their unaided reason. It is the birthright of the totalitarian tradition.

Paul Johnson[1]

There is no way I'm teaching that stuff!" my disgruntled colleague mumbled in the high school teachers' lounge. We were a part of a curriculum committee responsible for implementing a new program in the school district where we taught.

My troubled colleague went on to explain, "I reduced a six-inch stack of possible curriculum down to only one-quarter of one inch. All the rest was so liberally biased, if I taught it I'd be nothing but a propagandist for socialism."

As I began to investigate this new program I, too, became concerned. Something didn't seem right. I expanded my research and discovered that not only was my school district vigorously selling this program to teachers, but it was being introduced all across the country. It was to be the

15

newest and most ambitious vision the education community could address.

Teachers are natural visionaries; they have to be. It takes someone with vision to look at a room full of children, each having different backgrounds, influences, abilities, and learning styles and envision the next generation's doctors, business professionals, and productive mothers, fathers, and citizens. When Johnny teases his neighbor for the umpteenth time, it takes a visionary to see that someday Johnny will be a sensitive father of four children. Or when Sally can't seem to grasp even the simplest of math problems, it takes a dedicated visionary to see her as an astronaut in twenty years. Our society—in fact, the world—is indebted to teachers with vision.

Visionaries, however, can be vulnerable to those with greater vision. A teacher who has a vision for helping children grow up in an increasingly complex world can be vulnerable to an "expert" who has the ultimate vision for making the world a lovely Garden of Eden. Therein lies the danger. Visionaries are being sold the "ultimate" vision— perpetual peace and highest fulfillment on spaceship Earth. What a wonderful dream! Who would deny it is a noble ambition? If it could be brought about, it would represent the crowning achievement of educators. However, educators and the general public must fully examine the entire vision before buying into it.

The book of Proverbs observes that, "Where there is no vision, the people perish" (29:18). Our hopes, dreams, and ambitions are the fuel for life. Vision keeps us moving onward. Envisioning where we want to be in relation to God, our fellow man, and the world provides the framework in which we construct our life's journey. But vision alone is insufficient. Just any vision will not provide a brighter, healthier future.

When we think of a visionary, we often think of men and women of the past who led people to great heights in some particular area. We think of great statesmen, inventors, scientists, religious leaders, and business men and women. But we must remember that Hitler, Lenin, and Mao-Tse-tung also had visions. It could be argued that of all men they harbored the most grandiose visions—visions involving hatred, murder, oppression, and totalitarianism. So it is true that without a vision the people perish; it is also true that the people will perish if they have a deadly vision.

Public education is in danger of falling prey to a deadly vision. With all the flak that public schools are receiving over existing programs and policies, it would seem crazy to introduce a new program that will call down even more wrath from the American public. But many educators seem dead set on doing so.

In your community it may be called International Studies or Cultural Awareness or Futurism or any one of a dozen names. But Global Education involves a whole new philosophy of life—a philosophy that has no roots in mainstream American thought. Its proponents define it as having a *world-mindedness* or as seeing ourselves as components in a vast sea of humanity.

Though global education does involve some positive directions, it also endangers the security of our country and the faith of our children.

Leading global educators are seeking to formulate U.S. policy, not by using proper democratic channels, but by ensnaring the mind-set of future generations. When the general public realizes what these globalists are planning, the wrath of the people will not stop at removing just this one, specific program from the public school system. The leaders within the global movement are interested in public education only as a means to mold the public, not in education molded *by* the public.

For the sake of our country and our children, educators and parents must understand what global education is and what it promotes. It is a fatal vision, both for public education and for free people everywhere.

Definitions of Globalism

For most people, seeing that famous photograph of earth as viewed from the moon was the beginning of the realization that all humanity is riding a precariously balanced sphere in the middle of nowhere. Humankind may be divided on earth, but we are united as we whirl through space on this shared planet we call Earth. This perspective prompted educators to promote a global consciousness to enhance public education. There is no single definition of global education. Each global writer offers a slightly different meaning. Most often, writers use a potpourri of definitions to get the general idea across.

- "[E]fforts to bring about changes in the content, in the methods, and in the social context of education, in order to better prepare students for citizenship in the global age."[2]

- "[E]ducation for responsible citizenship in an increasingly interdependent society."[3]

- "[T]he realization that the earth is a single system; it is the process of being open, sensitive, knowledgeable and positive toward other cultures as well as toward one's own."[4]

- "[A]n effort to equip all citizens with the variety of skills and the range of knowledge needed to cope with worldwide economic, scientific, political, and intercultural realities and opportunities."[5]

Common themes in most definitions are the concepts of interdependence, cooperation, tolerance, empathy, internationalism, distribution of wealth, and selflessness.

Effective global education must be infused throughout the entire curriculum. It goes beyond mere social studies and is more intent on social attitude. To achieve this attitude it is vital that a global perspective permeate not only social studies, English, and science, but also math, physical education, music, auto shop, and drafting classes.

Other names for global education are: International Studies, Multicultural International Education, Global R.E.A.C.H. (Respecting our Ethnic And Cultural Heritage), Project 2000, Welcome to Planet Earth, and World Core Curriculum, to name just a few.

Justifications for Global Education

Advocates of global education clearly recognize the many problems facing our world and are attempting to help shape a better one by adjusting current perspectives to deal more intelligently with world problems as they see them.

Globalists stress that the world is becoming a smaller "global village," or as some refer to our planet, "spaceship Earth." We must deal with a host of international problems such as food shortages, poverty, population growth, worldwide pollution, the arms race, and terrorism. In all of these we are colliding with other cultural perspectives and must learn to adapt quickly for future interaction.

Prior to 1981 the majority of trade crossed the Atlantic Ocean to Europe. This was the pattern for over 300 years. Now more trade crosses the Pacific Ocean bound for ports along the Pacific rim. For the U.S., this has significance both economically and culturally. As economic interaction with the East increases so will cultural interaction, bringing a greater influx of Eastern music, art, philosophy, and religion into America.

American businesses compete not only with each other but also with companies in other countries. As this trend increases, international competition alone seems ample justification for a globally oriented curriculum.

To meet this challenge global educators want to promote positive learning such as:

- Cross-cultural understanding
- Attitudes of cooperation among people
- Friendliness and concern for others
- A sense of responsibility as to personal roles and the role of our country in a world of nations
- Proficiency in a second language
- Acquiring, analyzing, and using information
- Decision-making skills
- The ability to make judgments
- Cooperation, mediation, and conflict resolution skills

Could anyone be against these goals?

Educators sometimes use an overly simplistic logic when selecting various programs. This logic states that a program that says it solves a particular problem will most likely do so if its general goals are in order. The error in this type of thinking is that it rarely looks at the underlying philosophies along with the day-to-day methods used to achieve the stated goals.

Anyone who has been in education for very long can think of school districts that have sunk hundreds of thousands, even millions, of dollars into the latest "innovation" and after a few years dropped it because it never accomplished what it set out to do. And of course, those who opposed accepting the innovation were seen at that time as anti-education, backward, nonprogressive traditionalists.

We can safely assume that anyone with an ounce of intelligence would agree with the above stated goals of globalists. To think otherwise would mean promotion of cross-cultural misunderstanding, attitudes of divisiveness, hatred for others, irresponsibility, indecision, lack of judgment, and general stupidity.

The concern over global education does not center around these overly broad goals. It centers around the more specific objectives, the lack of balance in political viewpoints, the underlying philosophies of many global programs, as well as what might be called the ultimate goal of many globalists.

Before looking at the negative areas of current global education, it is important to address the positive aspects of the idea. Rarely is a program all bad or all good. Discernment is essential for wise instructional selection.

3

WHAT'S RIGHT ABOUT GLOBAL EDUCATION?

If it be possible, as much as lieth in you, live peacefully with all men.

Romans 12:18

It was my first year teaching, and I eagerly looked forward to introducing my ninth graders to the rich history of the world, specifically the Middle East. I spent several weeks teaching about the cultures, the languages, the foods, the wars, and so forth. Finally test time came. The children did well on all the questions but one: locate the Middle East on a map of the world. Over half the class failed. As the tests were collected, and I saw circles drawn around places like Japan, Sweden, and even Cuba, I realized one simple fact. In three weeks of teaching on the Middle East, I had never once showed the kids where in the world it was!

I must not have been alone in my rookie foible. Studies now abound from various organizations attesting to the sorry state of American children's world knowledge.

23

The need for improving current world-mindedness is vital among both children and adults. We have no choice but to prepare for the future in education. International relations and concerns are a reality with which we must deal. Globalist writer Lee Anderson makes a good point when he says: "Any real choice we may have once had in this matter is eroding, and the task of globalizing American education is rapidly entering into the kingdom of necessity where the only real choices center on how well and how rapidly the task gets executed."[1]

Our interactions with other nations and cultures will only increase in the years to come. How we prepare today will to a large degree determine how comfortably we live tomorrow. But the type of global education being proposed for schools must be carefully examined.

In my studies of global needs and global writers, I have identified four general areas which certainly need emphasis in American education.

Proficiency in a Second Language

Americans hold a unique and privileged position in the world. Due to our size, geographical isolation, and economic and political power in the world community, it has not been necessary for us to speak anything but English in order to survive. In fact, English is rapidly becoming the international language. However, as we interact with nations more intimately, it would create far better communication and cultural understanding if each of us would become proficient in a second language.

Currently schools only offer French, Spanish, or German as electives. Many colleges no longer require studies in foreign languages at all. Even when a language is learned, there often is little opportunity to practice it, and, thus, the skill is lost. This is not the fault of the school but more a result of our nation's size and relative isolation. Dutch students, in contrast, find it imperative to understand several languages. Their homeland is small, surrounded by other language groups, and highly international in its economy.

The study of another language is excellent for mental development and academic exercise, but we need language courses that are also relevant to current needs. Since it is true that the Pacific Ocean has become the field for international trade, should we not also offer Japanese or Mandarin Chinese? And since we would all like to see greater constructive dialogue with the Soviet Union, would it not be a good idea to study Russian?

Foreign language courses also could be enriched by concurrent study of the international economic relations between the U.S. and those countries. For example, since our trade with Korea will only increase, we should teach young people how to encourage America's economy by having them study trade relations with Korea.

Cultural Sensitivity

Global education calls for an increase in cultural sensitivity. Often the rise of conflict, both interpersonally and internationally, comes from intolerance. Millions have died because they were viewed by their conquerors as barbaric, savage, or suspiciously different.

Tolerance is a key ingredient of freedom. Of course, tolerance has its limits. I will tolerate your swinging your fist anywhere you desire, but my intolerance begins at the tip of my nose. Educators should instill an attitude of tolerance in their students. However, tolerance leads to lonely isolation unless it is followed by understanding, which is followed by respect, which is followed by appreciation.

Understanding means knowing why a person behaves or believes a certain way. More than simply accepting the fact that others have the right to be different, understanding involves knowing the motives behind the difference.

After a person's ways are understood, they can be respected. *Respect* has several definitions, but here it means to ascribe a dignity to another's customs. I can tolerate another person's action without understanding it or allowing them any dignity in my mind. That kind of tolerance is mere indifference. Respect, in this context, does not necessarily mean agreement or endorsement. It means that an action is understood to the point of allowing it to be carried out while giving it due dignity.

The final step in cultural sensitivity is *appreciation*, saying, "I'm glad you are acting or believing the way you do." It may involve the desire to adopt a particular custom or belief that is not indigenous to your own. For example, the Japanese love to eat raw fish. An American unaccustomed to this delicacy could tolerate a Japanese family's diet. After talking to them, he might understand that they eat it because they find it very delicious. If the American invited the family to a potluck, and they brought raw fish, he would show respect for their choice by not holding his nose or giving some other sign of disgust. And finally, he might try the dish and find that he also appreciates it.

Sensitivity to and respect for other cultures are highly valued characteristics of a well-rounded individual. They show an openness to new ideas and new ways of living. However, cultural sensitivity should not be confused with cultural relativity. Cultural relativity says that each culture operates on faith and not truth; each culture defines right and wrong, honor and shame, justice and injustice, mortal and divine based on its own context. Therefore, it cannot be judged by someone outside that cultural group. To do so would be, relativists say, ethnocentric and, thus, wrong. This, of course, runs counter to the Judeo-Christian concept of ultimate reality and would be dangerous, both ethically and legally, to teach in the public school classroom. Such teaching would come in direct conflict with the Judeo-Christian concepts of absolute moral principles—a belief held by many students.

Understanding the Impact of Policy

Students need to develop an understanding of the impact of U.S. foreign and domestic policies on the world. They should also sense the need for long-range goals and far-sighted planning in government policy.

This long-term view is difficult to acquire in our instant society. News is communicated in seconds. Dinners that once took hours to cook now take minutes. Documents were once written by hand; then came the typewriter, the electric typewriter, and now the word processor.

Combine the sense of the instantaneous with our political structure which is built around four-year presidential terms (with most people only remembering the last year of an incumbent's term or what the challenger will do for them tomorrow). The result? We speak of doing the expedient rather than the excellent thing.

We must help children see the need for patience rather than instant gratification, and the importance of long-range consequences rather than immediate payoff. This is especially important for helping students become responsible future voters. Students need to learn that domestic decisions affect the New York stock market, which in turn affects stock exchanges around the world. Social unrest in South Africa or Mexico sends shock waves throughout the world, both politically and economically.

International Trade and Economics

Globalists continually speak of interdependence in the world. This term is not artificial; *interdependence* is a description of the world as it is today. The U.S., for instance, is dependent on its allies to join in an economic boycott of a renegade nation. Other nations depend on a relationship with the U.S. to increase world political stability.

Interdependence is even more obvious in international trade and manufacturing. Computer parts come from Japan or Taiwan as well as the Silicon Valley. Educators frequently use a simple illustration of global interdependence—"The World in a Chocolate Bar." This worksheet shows that the ingredients in a chocolate bar come from around the world.

Often educators tend to show trade and economics from a governmental and political view; students must also learn the positive achievements and exciting future in international business and free market principles. Great business men and women should be held up as role models for young people. As young people have confidence in the opportunities of business and as they see that principles of capitalism fuel a free society, they can extend themselves boldly into transnational relationships. Can anyone deny the interdependence that the world shares? The question is not whether it exists but how we will function in it.

These, then, are the four general areas necessary for learning to function well in the future international scene. This need not assume a liberal one-worldness. I am merely saying certain international trends are obvious, and we need to look for the best ways of coping with those trends. We must learn how to deal with international relations on many levels. Believing that our national makeup and our relations with the world are still the same as they were two hundred years ago is simplistic. It is, however, equally unrealistic to view loyalty to the nationalistic aspirations of the framers of our Constitution as antiquated and ineffective for the future.

We must safeguard our public schools against narrow political bias as well as psychologically oriented therapy/education and spiritual, sectarian influences. All these are present in global education as it is currently being offered to school districts. Every educator, parent, and student must become aware of these patterns and act appropriately.

Global educators have a vision, but it is a tunnel vision. It is extremely narrow-minded, yet ironically claims to be open-minded. When all is said and done, globalists allow no other alternative to total acceptance of their particular viewpoint.

First, globalists paint a morbid, disaster-ridden picture of the "inevitable" future; then they offer one solution—their solution—as viable. Children are backed into an intellectual corner and then, given no other alternative, must surrender to globalistic ideology.

Global education has four major weaknesses. These weaknesses, however, form the very foundation for the globalists' New Age, utopian vision. Global education crowds out the study of Western civilization; it teaches that there are no absolutes; it seeks to politically resocialize students into liberal extremism. Some global educators preach a new religion for the world based on Eastern mysticism. In fact, global education is the political side of the New Age coin.

Globalists claim that these four elements are essential to bringing about peace and world prosperity. In light of that, it is doubtful that they will allow these aspects to be touched, but it is precisely here that global education poses the greatest threat to the individual, public schools, and society.

PART TWO

THE POLITICS
BEHIND THE MASK

4

ONE WORLD CULTURE: NO MORE WESTERN CIVILIZATION

Culture of intellect, without religion in the heart, is only civilized barbarism and disguised animalism.

Bunsen

The third-grade girl in a small town in Wisconsin had worked hard on her construction paper Valentine's card. Each letter was carefully drawn. The picture on the front was meticulously colored in crayon. *The teacher will surely be proud of this*, she must have been thinking as she finished her masterpiece. But when the teacher saw it, the little girl was told to do it over; it was not acceptable.

The child had written at the top, "I Love Jesus," and that phrase could not be displayed alongside the other children's artwork. Or at least that is why, the teacher explained, the child would have to stay in during recess and cover up the offensive phrase. "This is a public school," the teacher said, as if that ended all discussion on the matter.

There is an increasing sense among public school teachers that any expression of religious faith in public schools cannot be tolerated, even the gentle expression of a child. I wonder if that little girl had been from a Third World country and had written of her devotion to another god, if the teacher would have seen that as a wonderful opportunity for "classroom cultural enrichment." Unfortunately, global education encourages that kind of unequal treatment.

Globalists frequently speak of understanding other cultures and feeling a part of the world culture *after* being well grounded in one's own culture. But in the enthusiasm to bring a broad range of foreign cultures to young people, we are neglecting our Western heritage. We assume that since students live in the Western world, they unconsciously absorb Western cultural ideals.

In many schools, world history courses are given greater importance than courses in Western civilization. In an effort to teach about as many African and Asian cultures as possible, we leave little time for a quality study of Greek and Roman history, the rise of Christianity, the development of Europe, the significance of the Roman Catholic Church, the glory of the Renaissance, and the impact of the Reformation. Because of this, events of Western history become stereotyped and are reduced to items fit for a trivia game. And confusingly, European history is frequently taught within the context of African or Asian history. Thus, teachers spend an unbalanced amount of time emphasizing European colonization and exploitation of Third World regions, giving students a skewed perception of the value of Western history.

Melting Pots and Salad Bowls

American children are, for the most part, products and reflections of Western civilization. A black American student in Detroit does not have the perspective of an African student. An Asian American student, for all practical purposes, looks at life in the same way as most American students. To believe that an American with a particular ethnic heritage will hold the same values as a native of his mother country just because of the racial similarity is a type of inverted racism.

Of course, each ethnic group in America brings unique and enriching qualities to our culture, and this enrichment should always be encouraged. However, in spite of our racial diversity, we, as Americans, reflect certain ideals and philosophies that are definitely products of Western civilization. Our system of government and administration of justice are products of Western thinking. Our scientific mind-set is Western. Our economic values and market structure reflect Western values. There are blacks, Asians, and Hispanics in large numbers who share the same religion: Christianity.

Western cultural values are interracial; they provide the common bond between diverse groups—our unity in diversity. I applaud the study of many cultures in our schools, but we must give more than lip service to the idea of grounding students in Western cultural values. If we neglect the teaching of our American commonalities by solely emphasizing our ethnic diversity, we will have no unity amidst our diversity. Educators like to speak of the concept of a melting pot being outmoded, calling a salad bowl a better depiction of our nation's ethnic diversity. We must not forget, however, that our Western cultural heritage is the bowl that keeps us together in our wonderful diversity. To teach multicultural education without upholding Western cultural values is like trying to eat a delectable salad that is floating helter-skelter in a weightless atmosphere.

The Disappearance of Christianity

The U.S. Department of Education commissioned Dr. Paul C. Vitz of New York University to conduct an extensive survey entitled "Religion and Traditional Values in Public School Textbooks." The results of his study revealed how one aspect of Western culture, Christianity, is being addressed in textbooks today.

> The dominant theme is the denial of religion as an actual important part of American life. Sometimes the censorship becomes especially offensive. It is common in these books to treat Thanksgiving without explaining to whom the Pilgrims gave thanks.
>
> The Pueblo can pray to Mother Earth, but Pilgrims can't be described as praying to God—and never are Christians described as praying to Jesus either in the United States or elsewhere, in the present or even in the past.[1]

In reference to world history textbooks, Vitz systematically lists the omissions of significant portions of Western civilization. He lists one book that:

> . . . [H]as twenty pages on Tanzania and nineteen pages on the history of the Netherlands; sixteen pages on ancient Crete. It makes no reference to Martin Luther and Calvin and there is almost nothing on Protestantism. The absence of reference to Protestantism in Holland is particularly noteworthy given that country's history.
>
> One of the strange characteristics of many of the texts was their failure to mention the Protestant Reformation, or to give it very little emphasis.
>
> This neglect of Protestantism further supports the thesis that some kind of repression or denial of Christianity (especially Protestantism) is demonstrated by how these texts treat the Christian religion.[2]

Earlier in his study Vitz states that "those responsible for these books appear to have a deep-seated fear of any form of active contemporary Christianity, especially serious, committed Protestantism. This fear has led the authors to deny and repress the importance of this kind of religion in American life."[3]

Concerning Judeo-Christian influences on world history, Vitz comments:

> To appreciate the neglect of the life of Jesus it is only necessary to compare it with some books' coverage of the life of Mohammed. In several books Mohammed's life gets much more coverage than that of Jesus. For example, consider Silver-Burdett: the life of Jesus gets 36 lines, while the life of Mohammed gets 104 lines; Riverside mentions Mohammed as founder of Islam . . . but Jesus is not mentioned anywhere in the text. . . . Islam gets much positive coverage in Laidlaw. . . . Specifically, the rise of Islam, Islamic culture and Mohammed get an eleven-page section plus other scattered coverage. The rise of Christianity gets almost nothing (e.g., a few lines on p. 116). In these books it is not as though great religious figures are totally avoided—it is rather that Jesus is.
>
> Catholicism is simply excluded from U.S. history from 1800 to the present.
>
> The early history of the Jews is of foundational significance to the West; in many respects it is as important as ancient Greece and more important than ancient Egypt. However, there is far less coverage of Jewish history than of either Egypt or Greece in most of these books. Certainly the origin of monotheism, the stories of Abraham, Moses, David, and the prophets . . . are central to Western life and history, indeed to much of Islam as well.
>
> There is no reference to Jewish life and culture in the last 2000 years—until the WWII holocaust. In other words, the Judeo part of the Judeo-Christian history of the West is far from adequately represented.[4]

When referring to the coverage of Spanish Christianity in Mexico, Vitz says,

> Some important treatment of Christianity is clearly anti-Christian. . . . There is no balanced treatment which would include the positive contributions of Christianity to the Indians, no critical comment on Indian religion, for example the very prevalent human sacrifice among Mexican Indians.[5]

The last segment of his study is devoted to an analysis of the focus of third- and sixth-grade basal readers. Dr. Vitz concludes by stating, "The above characteristics taken together make it clear that these basal readers are so written as to represent a systematic denial of the history, heritage, beliefs, and values of a very large segment of the American people."[6]

Dr. Vitz's study is of great importance as it clearly reveals that a significant aspect of Western civilization is not being passed on to future generations. The de-emphasis of our Western culture is a recurring theme among global educators.

Some globalists apparently want a new world culture to arise out of a blending of many diverse cultures. If this is not explicit in their writings, it certainly is implicit. For example, Bruce R. Joyce and Alexander M. Nicholson of Stanford University write:

> We wonder whether a transnational culture . . . is possible today, whether there can be any common ground for a world society in which the various nations and peoples participate while maintaining their separate identities. . . . We want the answer to be yes; but the answer will be yes if, and only if, the imperatives for global education are carried out.[7]

Many globalists desire a new culture that is identifiable by its fluidity. This new culture sees truth as relative to context and need and can thus accept and reject aspects of many cultures as the individual so desires. Rick L. Hamblin expresses this when he writes:

> The term *transcultural* refers to the individual's opportunity and ability to select characteristics from one or more cultures to design and develop one's own individuality. This definition clearly establishes the intent of the rationale: to enhance individualism through the education process of synthesizing cultural options.[8]

Remember, though, that in the midst of all this cross-cultural blending, the individual is to be well rooted in his or her own cultural heritage. My cultural heritage is Western and more specifically, American. How well will those values be inculcated in my children by their schools? I am an American. I think like an American, and I bring with me a lot of cultural baggage accumulated over thousands of years. My ethnic heritage is Swiss and Irish, but my intellectual heritage is Greek and Roman, while my moral and religious heritage is Jewish and Christian. I do not care much about my ethnic heritage, but I place a tremendous importance on my roots in Greek, Roman, Jewish, and Christian culture. So if my children are to be well grounded in their cultural heritage, they will need to know the fundamentals of Western civilization.

Cultural Fairs

Cultural fairs are becoming popular in multicultural programs. A school holding such a fair encourages children to study their own heritage and create displays reflecting their personal backgrounds. Most often these events really are not cultural fairs as much as they are ethnic fairs. To truly reflect the majority of American children's cultural heritage, regardless of race, they would need to display the works of Plato, Aristotle, Moses, Jesus, the Apostle Paul, Cicero, Augustine, Dante, Locke, Michelangelo, De Vinci, Martin Luther, Thomas Jefferson, and many other Western influences.

Global educators would have us forget the study of the past—Western heritage—and move on to more enlightened frontiers of learning. H. G. Vonk reflected this thinking in a 1973 article: "Back in the social studies classroom, pupils are being readied for the crucial challenge via guided tours through the historical dustbin. The dead issues of the distant, cold past are marched in and out of the classroom like so many obedient soldiers."[9] With that kind of thinking in our schools, we are in danger of forever losing any hope of a grounding in our true cultural heritage, Western civilization.

In the name of teaching many cultures of the world to develop world-mindedness, global education diminishes a true education in the great cultural heritage of which all Americans partake. Whether you are black, white, Asian, or Hispanic, and whether you like it or not, if you live in America you are tremendously impacted by Western history. And for the most part the vast majority of Americans enjoy the benefits of that heritage. Our public schools should be helping students understand it to a greater degree so they can continue to reap the benefits.

CULTURAL RELATIVITY: NO MORE ABSOLUTES

Humanity is ready for a new culture.

Dr. Robert Muller

A mother came up to me after I addressed an audience of parents in Lowell, Indiana, concerning the importance of reforming public schools. Her story touched me deeply.

While her son was in the eighth grade, she and her husband decided to talk to him about sex, AIDS, and homosexuality. When the parents mentioned that some of his friends may someday choose immoral sexual behavior, even homosexuality, the boy reacted strongly and emphasized that he would not even associate with those types of people.

One year later, after the boy completed a ninth-grade health class, the parents found themselves in another discussion with their son regarding human sexuality. "This time he had an equally strong reaction," the mother related to me with tears in her eyes, "but he told us that his values may not be our values and that we certainly couldn't push our morality on any of his friends. Everyone takes his own path to right and wrong."

This incident highlights the prevalent philosophy taught in public schools today: *relativism*—the belief that no absolute moral principles exist. New Age globalism also emphasizes this notion.

As was pointed out earlier, cultural sensitivity and cultural relativity are quite different. However, in the name of sensitivity, globalists actually encourage relativity. Their logic goes something like this: "In the future we will be faced with many situations in which we will need to promote harmony and cooperation. Since this is needed for survival in the global village, we must abandon the separatist notion of absolutes. Absolutes lock us into conflict-oriented relationships and do not allow for compromise. Acceptance of ambiguity will be a valued attitude for future generations."

Lynda Falkenstein of the Northwest Regional Educational Laboratory outlines this philosophy under the heading, "Critical Attributes of Global Education."

> Ambiguity. Black-and-white answers probably never really existed but the time is long past even the myth can endure. Competent world citizens must act in the large zone of grays where absolutes are absent. The grays are made up of difficult and conflicting values where one right challenges another. Tolerance for ambiguity is essential at all ages and positions in life.[1]

Black-and-white answers do not exist at all? Ambiguity must be accepted in all positions in life? This would then include law and justice, personal morality, and international integrity. This is situational ethics on a cultural scale. Falkenstein's thinking constitutes a philosophy of life antithetical to mainstream American thought, yet she lists this as a critical part of global education.

Global Education and Values Clarification

M. Frances Klein and Kenneth A. Tye of the Institute for Development of Educational Activities (I.D.E.A.) state that, "values clarification is . . . an important component" of global education.[2] Values clarification, as developed by Louis Raths and Sidney Simons, is based entirely on situational ethics. This ethical system assumes there are no transcendent absolute principles by which decisions can be made. Ethics are determined only by circumstances at hand, consequences desired, and personal feelings.

In the book *Learning for Tomorrow: The Role of the Future in Education*, Wendell Bell goes even further in explaining how man will cope with what Falkenstein calls *ambiguity*.

[T]he demise of superstition and cultural "absolutes," if they die, may unshackle humankind for presently unknown purposes. As [Fredrik] Polack says: 'In setting himself purposefully to control and alter the course of events man has been forced to deal with concepts of value, means, and ends, ideals and ideologies, as he has attempted to blueprint his own future. As long as the prophet-propitiator was acting only as a divine transmitter of messages from on high, man felt that he was accepting this ethics ready-made, with no alterations allowed. In a latter stage man staggers under the double load of not only having to construct his own future but having to create the values which will determine its design.'[3]

Bell states we will create our best destiny by freeing ourselves from the shackles of absolutes and jumping headlong into the admittedly ambiguous realm of relativism.

We would be wise to listen to men like Gerald H. Paske, associate professor of philosophy at Wichita State University, who comments that "the new approaches to moral education—such as values clarification and moral development—have failed or, at best they have not been particularly successful."[4] William Kirk Kirkpatrick, associate professor of educational psychology at Boston College, points out that, "If social and moral judgments are nothing more than preferences, the preferences of those with the loudest voices and the most push will come to prevail."[5]

In one global program entitled *Welcome to Earth: Culture Study Handbook for Elementary Schools*, cultural relativism is stated to be the underlying philosophy of the lessons. In the preface the designers quote Kurt Vonnegut, Jr. stating:

> I've often thought there ought to be a manual to hand to little kids, telling them what kind of planet they're on, why they don't fall off it, how much time they've probably got here, how to avoid poison ivy, and so on. I would call it WELCOME TO EARTH. One thing I would really like to tell them about is cultural relativity. . . . A first grader should understand that his or her culture isn't a rational invention; that there are thousands of other cultures and they all work pretty well; that all cultures function on faith rather than truth; that there are lots of alternatives to our own society. Cultural relativity is defensible and attractive. It's also a source of hope. It means we don't have to continue this way if we don't like it.[6]

Cultural relativity is not defensible nor is it attractive. If we truly believed that moral truth was relative according to culture, then we could not raise a voice against slavery, apartheid, male chauvinism, or any one of a dozen "cultural" barbarities. Erwin Lutzer raises this point in his book, *The Necessity of Ethical Absolutes*, when he states: "[W]e must ask whether the cultural facts warrant the moral theory drawn from them. . . . By what step of reasoning is it possible to move from what is to what *ought to be*? Cultural facts can never lead us to the *ought* of moral responsibility."[7]

The fact that South Africa has practiced the principles of apartheid for three hundred years, making it a centerpiece of white South African custom and belief, does not lend credibility to the immorality of the act. Are we now going to teach children that apartheid is acceptable in certain cultures? According to Falkenstein we must accept such moral ambiguities.

She states that, "Black-and-white answers probably never really existed but the time is long past even the myth can endure." This means that there really is no answer to the question of whether apartheid is right or wrong. She goes on, "Competent world citizens must act in the large zone of grays where absolutes are absent." Would she also include the absolute value of human life, racial equality, and the right to life, liberty, and the pursuit of happiness? She continues, "The grays are made up of difficult and conflicting values [to have apartheid or not to have it] where one right challenges another [the white minority government v. the black people]." She concludes that we must look the other way and not pass judgment on this culture that has "conflicting values" with our own. As she states, "Tolerance for ambiguity is essential at all ages and positions in life." This would include teachers and congressmen.

Such an acceptance of relativism is ludicrous and would not help the world situation at all. In fact, it would give moral license to the Pol Pots and Khomeinis of our world. As long as these madmen could show a cultural basis for their actions, we would have to tolerate their barbarities.

Professor Allan Bloom in his best-selling book, *The Closing of the American Mind*, criticizes such "open-minded" thinking, observing that:

> The point is to force students to recognize that there are other ways of thinking and that Western ways are not better. It is again not the content that counts but the lesson to be drawn. Such requirements are part of the effort to establish a world community and train its members—the person devoid of prejudice. But if students were really to learn something of the minds of any of these non-Western cultures—which they don't—they would find that each

and every one of these cultures is ethnocentric. All of them think their way is the best way, and all others are inferior.[8]

Global writers stress the essential nature of cultural relativity as a major plank in the global education platform. The danger is that, on the surface, these underlying philosophies are not immediately apparent. For instance, although the preface in the program "Welcome to Earth: Culture Study Handbook for Elementary Schools" refers to the need for cultural relativism, the rest of the program seems quite harmless. It speaks of the many people on our planet, of people's similar basic needs, of what goes into making a culture, and so on. A curriculum review committee could easily give a superficial reading of the material and totally miss the ideological basis for the program. Though the initial lessons seem harmless, the ideological undertow advances the philosophy that all cultures are basically alike—no one is better. A review committee must ask itself where this program will lead in five years with an ideological bias that believes there are no absolutes.

The Evil of Thinking You Are Right

Another danger is that global writers describe their goals using terms with which everyone would agree. Further reading of the author's intent reveals that relativism, again, is the desired product. For instance, James Becker, a leader in the push for global education writes in his book, *Schooling for a Global Age,* that basic academic skills should be taught in "world-centered" schools, those having global education in full swing. Among those skills he lists: "The skills of comparison, analysis, inquiry, and the capacity to make rational judgments." Nobody would disagree with that goal, but his next sentence sheds new light: "This skill includes learning modes of thinking that are relatively free from egocentric and ethnocentric perceptions."[9]

This is another way of saying that an individual's moral conscience, the basis for rational judgments, is slanted by egocentric and ethnocentric influences and must be freed from this to accept culturally diverse ideas of what is truth. In other words, a child should not believe too strongly in anything in order to be free from egocentric and ethnocentric bias.

We see an example of how this filters into the classroom in one worksheet entitled "Washington and the World," handed out at an educator's conference hosted by the Port of Seattle. The worksheet dealt with the issue of *ethnocentrism*, defined as the tendency for people to believe that their culture, religion, race, or nation is superior and to judge others by one's own frame of reference. It instructed the teacher to make a series of statements while the students identified the ethnocentric ones. Facts were mixed with opinions and the opinions were marked as ethnocentric. Included in the statements was the sentence, "Christianity has a more practical code of ethics than Hinduism." This was listed as ethnocentric. While it is true that the statement is ethnocentric—it judges others based on a particular religious viewpoint—a Christian child who believes the Bible is the absolute basis for ethics would say the statement is a fact, not an opinion. Since globalists believe that ethnocentrism is the great evil of the world, the Christian student would not do well in a "world-centered school."

Other statements which would intrude on beliefs held by child and family are, "An Indian says, 'Those Americans are immoral; they eat cows.'" and "A Christian says, 'Hindus who believe in reincarnation are wrong and will be punished by God.'" What if a Hindu student were in the class? The teacher has just taught that his belief in the sacredness of cows is not absolutely true at all; it is only cultural, ethnocentric. The same intrusion would occur with the Christian child. Basically, the teacher would be presenting a religious view—all truth is relative to culture. The implication is that if you believe it to be a fact that Hindus will be punished by God, you are an ethnocentric bigot. Schools should not be in the business of challenging family-taught religious beliefs.

Some might argue that the teacher is taking no religious stand but is open to all stands, but this in itself is a stand. Remember the old saying, "To decide not to decide is a decision." Cultural relativism is a religious view. It deals with the nature of ultimate reality by answering that each culture is right and no one can be wrong. Cultural sensitivity, on the other hand, would stress the importance of having a tolerant attitude toward foreign ideas, but it would not teach that truth must be ambiguous.

Globalism is more than an extended curriculum for world history and current events classes. It introduces a whole new philosophy of life to our children. Should we American taxpayers fund a program that has teachers telling children that their family's religion is not really the truth, that the only real truth is that everyone has the truth?

Teachers as Change Agents

Harold G. Shane and June Grant Shane, in their chapter entitled "Educating the Youngest for Tomorrow," comment that: "To accept the idea of a future-oriented education is to enter the ranks of those who believe that education must be an agent of cultural change."[10] Global education has rejected the notion that public education is the transmitter of a culture's established values and instead seeks to actively reshape our culture to conform to their vision of the future.

In June of 1968 the Washington State Superintendent of Public Instruction hosted a statewide education conference called to discuss the problems of youth. In the printed proceedings under the heading "Moral Values: Decadence or Redefinition" was this statement: "How do you involve young people in dialogue about questions of morality? . . . Maybe we need to get the children *out* of the home [experience in Israel was cited]. . . . not convinced that the home is always the best place to raise children!"[11]

What was a long-range goal in 1968 became an option in 1985. A 1985 report stated: "Consideration should be given to the establishment of a residential school or schools, perhaps similar to those of North Carolina, for highly capable high school students."[12] At that time North Carolina was looking at adopting statewide global education. In such a total global-oriented environment, the students could be more easily influenced in their moral perspectives.

Falkenstein freely admits to the frontal assault global education will have on traditional values:

> Global education is clearly not value free. It is openly and explicitly committed to a range of value goals evidenced in the preceding list of critical attributes [which included cultural relativity]. This feature is especially significant as we consider issues relevant to successfully implementing global education—not an add-on curriculum but a perspective infused into all aspects of current curriculum.[13]

In the rush to solve the world's problems, educators (or change agents, as Falkenstein refers to them) need to seriously consider the role global writers are demanding they assume. The evidence is overwhelmingly clear: you cannot become a global educator without becoming a moral relativist who actively preaches that dogma. There is a vast difference between being a world history or geography teacher and being a global educator.

An important consideration here is whether or not it is ethical to accept funding from American taxpayers who think educators are perpetuating their values, when all

along these educators are seeking to radically alter the
minds of the taxpayers' children. Why not first put these
new values to a vote? If the American people vote to have
their values changed, then educators could have a clear conscience about teaching this material. Teachers should be
above using the back door to politically resocialize children.

Again, Professor Allan Bloom comments:

> It is important to emphasize that the lesson the students
> are drawing from their studies is simply untrue. History
> and the study of cultures do not teach or prove that values
> or cultures are relative. All to the contrary, that is a philo-
> sophical premise that we now bring to our study of them.
> This premise is unproven and dogmatically asserted for
> what are largely political reasons.[14]

POLITICAL RESOCIALIZATION: NO MORE PATRIOTISM

We view global education as what sociologists call a "social movement." It is a new way of thinking about relationships in our world. As such, it has to seem legitimate to people and not to contradict current and deeply held values.

Ken Tye[1]

I sat in the crowded seminar as a representative from the United Nations began her presentation. "It's important that children get a sense of context when talking about world hunger and poverty," she explained. To do this she recommended that the teachers use large poster board and M&M candies. On each poster board we were to draw stick-figured people to represent the population of a different country. Below the figures of people we were then instructed to glue on the candies proportional to the amount of food available in that country. The poster for China was crowded with stick-figured people with only a few candies at the bottom. Ethiopia had only a few people, but it was allocated only one candy. The poster representing the United States had a moderate number of people but was crowded with candies.

The United Nations' instructor went on to exhort us to show children the vast inequity in food distribution around the world. The implications of what this instructor wanted taught were obvious. Unable to stand the one-sided lesson on international distribution of wealth, I raised my hand to ask a question. "Don't you think we should point out to the children that many of these countries have Marxist governments whose policies cause the severe shortage of food?" The presenter appeared flustered. She swept the comment aside with a curt acknowledgment of my point. "That may be something you could do," she said.

Tunnel vision is most pronounced among globalists when it comes to political education. They are propagandizing their narrow view of how the future should be. This is done by adopting a philosophy of education that focuses on how they think the world should be rather than teaching the reality of how it is. Of course, they argue that by barraging children with the doom-and-gloom scenarios they are portraying the world as it is. Obviously there are problems in the world, but globalists use the problems to build a case for their agenda. At the end of the globalist-guided journey, there is only one solution—theirs.

Falkenstein comments:

> Related to the issue of "change readiness" is the concept that people change when they are dissatisfied with a present condition. . . . The global education innovation must identify very specific and concrete ways of showing others how this product will be an improvement over what currently exists.[2]

This is why globalists are constantly introducing educators to their program by reciting a long list of current problems and explaining that we are totally unprepared to face these crises.

Global education, by design, must tear down America—tearing down American achievements so that the "new innovation" (globalism) will look appealing. Many teachers will not consciously do this, but the very nature of the program demands it. This is reflected by writers such as Richard Gross when he states the "global perspective stresses the increasing interdependence of nations, global hunger and poverty, population problems, worldwide pollution, nuclear warfare, and solutions."[3]

This is fairly typical—always the list of world problems and then the solution. But it is generally a politically liberal solution at the expense of a balanced education. Problems, problems, problems. It is no wonder that children today have anxiety about their future; they anticipate one full of crisis and despair.

Liberal Politics Liberally Taught

More educators need to seriously question the ideology behind "the solutions." Most often a review committee is pressured with a crisis mentality. They are led to believe that if the programs are not implemented immediately, their district might as well forget helping children cope with the future.

Note the inadequacies of the capitalistic system assumed by globalist Anna L. Rose Hawkes. In an outline of our world heritage, she suggests that high school students be taught that: "Differences among people today have been shaped by historical forces such as the industrial revolution, imperialism, and nationalism."[4] Nowhere does she mention the differences among people being shaped by Communist revolution, repression, and totalitarianism.

Global educators hate nationalism on the one hand, yet also claim they are not attacking patriotism. The *New Lexicon Webster's Dictionary* defines *nationalism* as "a devotion to one's nation, advocacy of national unity and independence." It defines *patriotism* as "a zealous love of one's country." In essence there is little difference, but global educators find it easier to attack *nationalism* rather than *patriotism* because it does not stir the same emotional response.

One might ask, "To what are we going to change once we are 'change ready'?" Globalist Richard MacLeod answers that question.

[W]e must change from . . . nationalism to internationalism. . . . We can internationalize our curriculum; we can internationalize the thinking and teaching of our staff and hopefully we can in time through the education process internationalize the students, our future leaders.[5]

Notice that academic freedom of thought is not even assumed here. Globalists like MacLeod demand that teachers not only teach internationalism but also *think* internationalism.

Lee Anderson goes even further when describing how he would like to see us change. He writes that students need to:

[R]ecognize that vast inequalities in the distribution of such human values as wealth, health, education, and respect are incapable of moral justification, and to accept the necessity for social polity aimed at reducing the gap between the rich and the poor both within and among nations.[6]

His use of the word *polity* is significant. Polity means a form of government, not a *policy* of government. In essence, Anderson is calling for a new—and obviously socialistic—form of government.

The activities of The Institute for Global Education of Grand Rapids, Michigan, is an example of leftist propaganda being sold as global education. Their magazine, *Eq-*

uity, contains a calendar of events listing only liberal political activities. For example, in one issue are listed "Equal Rights Amendment Rally," [Nuclear] "Freeze Party," "Rally and March for Disarmament," "Blockade the Bombers," "Commemoration of Soweto Massacre." The next year *Equity* listed more supposed global education activities including: "Freeze Walk-a-thon," "El Salvador Vigil," and a "Potluck to Commemorate the Anniversary of Sandinista Victory Over Somoza/U.S. Oppression."[7]

The masquerade of liberal politics thrust upon children in the name of world-mindedness could not be more pronounced.

Patriotism Has Got to Go

According to Falkenstein, globalists believe that any teacher holding firm cultural and patriotic convictions is unfit to teach in a school adopting global education. It should be noted that her work is a commentary on the common ideals set forth by over twenty of the nation's leading global educators. She reveals an absolute intolerance for teachers even thinking about alternatives to global education and points out the need for "reshaping many teacher's attitudes and beliefs about the world. It is unlikely that an individual holding highly ethnocentric and nationalistic views will be able to offer students opportunities for learning about pluralism, interdependence, and other concepts central to effective global education."[8]

This type of reasoning should offend every educator. Globalists bluntly state that teachers are unfit to think for themselves and that their attitudes and beliefs about the world must be reshaped. And if a teacher does not conform to a globalist's political viewpoint, then he or she is unfit to teach. The phrase, "[not] able to offer students opportunities for learning" is euphemistic for "unfit to teach" once a school's curriculum has converted to globalism.

> Virtually every educational innovation requires some re-training on the part of teachers within the system. Global education is different only in degree. It requires massive re-education by nearly everyone associated with the curriculum development and/or instructional process. . . . Because the threads in global education are laden with commitments which may mean value change for some people, the re-education process is more complex than simply teaching a technical process associated with reading or science.[9]

According to Falkenstein, the proper implementation of global education requires the "re-education" of all teachers. She is not talking about re-educating teachers about techniques or styles, but rather on what they believe about the world, how they think about political issues, and values they may hold dear. That is why she admits that the re-education process is complex.

Professor Allan Bloom comments that the recently graduated high school students who sit in his college courses are the products of political resocialization. "There is one thing a professor can be absolutely certain of: almost every student entering the university believes, or says he believes, that truth is relative. . . . The students, of course, cannot defend their opinion. It is something with which they have been indoctrinated."[10]

Targets of Resocialization

Teacher educators recognize that global education is controversial and will be met with opposition. But they believe that simple clarity in its introduction into a school system will defuse the controversy. Two prominent educators identify five structural elements which need to be in place before any innovation can be successfully brought about in a school:

1. Clarity on the part of the staff about the innovation

2. Capability of the staff to perform a new role model

3. Availability of necessary resources

4. Compatible organizational arrangements

5. Staff motivation

But the real question of ideological conflict has not been addressed. They assume that a teacher's objections to global education will only arise from misunderstanding or improper planning. What if a teacher fully understands global education and does not agree with it? The only solution to any objection is increased resocialization, more palatably called re-education. If re-education doesn't convert the teacher to global ideology, then, according to Falkenstein, that teacher would be unfit to teach and most likely replaced.

Teachers and children are not the only targets for resocialization. Capturing the mind-set of everyone in the nation is global education's ultimate goal. Leading global advocate and former Dean of UCLA's Graduate School of Education John Goodlad states: "Parents and the general public must be reached also. Otherwise, children and youth enrolled in globally oriented programs may find themselves in conflict with values assumed in the homes. And then the educational institution frequently comes under scrutiny and must pull back."[11]

Three startling things are revealed in Goodlad's statement. First, global educators are seeking to change the basic foundations of our entire culture. Second, the values parents teach their children are unashamedly attacked when the child gets to school. And third, the educational institution has no intention of responding properly to society's monitoring of the school curriculum. When a spotlight uncovers the covert ideology of global education, the globalist merely scurries to a dark corner to wait for the light to pass.

The relationship between community and teacher is built on a good faith. Statements like Goodlad's show a total disregard for that relationship. Such an attitude will only infuriate parents and promote bitter conflict between parent and teacher. The unfortunate thing is that although most teachers want to operate in an environment of good faith, they unwittingly become pawns in the hands of social engineers. The teachers, not the social engineers, will bear the brunt of parental anger for participating in this attempt at social reconstruction matched only by totalitarian regimes.

Changing the Minds of the Young

Of course, the modification of human behavior and attitudes must begin at an early age. Globalists point out that by the time children enter school they have many attitudes already established from the home. Globalist Edith W. King writes that: "The social education of the child in a world society and for a worldwide culture can begin in the early years."[12]

This is why Harold and June Shane in *Schooling for a Global Age* suggest that global education begin with children under the age of three. This sheds light on possible motives behind legislation for public school day-care centers. While many mothers may be helped by such a convenient state-run day-care program, educators seeking to alter children's attitudes would also be benefited.

To bring about attitudinal change in preschool children, Falkenstein insists that:

> The serious global educator and/or change agent will need to create wholly new links between the innovation and the informal structure(s) that influence development of attitudes and knowledge. This may include enlisting support from local community groups and educating them about global education while gaining their support

for it. At the very least, it must include attention to the source of student's attitudes and behaviors.[13]

Notice that globalists plan to gain local support *while* they educate the community about the program. It is significant that local support is not enlisted *after* the community understands global education. In other words, the community is pushed into giving credibility to a philosophy before it fully understands it.

Generally global initiators hold a few public meetings to tell parents and the general public about this exciting new program which is designed to make us once again competitive on the world market or to help us understand the problems behind cultural and political conflict in the world. If the school district's community is involved with international trade to *any* degree, initiators sell global education as a means of helping children survive in the international economic scene. Many times they highlight the influx of immigrants to an area to show that we as a people are so diverse that all cultures and all values must be promoted in our schools.

Your Town: A Gateway to the World

When I lived in Seattle, global educators there labeled our area the "gateway to the world." Later, I moved to Orange County, California, and found that global proponents there where saying the same thing. On a recent trip to Nebraska, a friend of mine heard globalists in that state claiming that Nebraska was the "heartland gateway to the world."

To globalists, every community that has a school targeted for global education is a "gateway to the world." Global educators play on the provincial attitudes of people. After all, no one wants their community to be considered insignificant. I suppose that if Mary's Igloo, Alaska, was targeted for global education, a case would be made for why it is the gateway to the world.

Falkenstein offers a footnote to the above information to explain the "source of student's attitudes and behaviors."

> The sources referred to here are key agents influencing political socialization of young people. Some of them include television, movies, and newspapers. In addition to media agents, the influence of "heroes" and highly visible figures must also be considered. Research supports the hypotheses that visibility lends credibility to a position regardless of what it is.[14]

Globalists have already done all the thinking for us and now just need the right "highly visible" people to get children to buy into global political socialization. These narrow political views do not need to be tested in the open arena of the classroom because, with the right "heroes" promoting it, their "visibility lends credibility to a position regardless of what it is."

When referring to "attitudinal obstacles," James Becker laments:

> Elementary school children's sense of belonging to a national political community is established and reinforced by many symbols. The global political community lacks such readily available symbols; the U.N. flag, for example, is known to only a small proportion of young children. . . . [F]or most children membership in a world community is not fostered with the same intensity or consensus by socialization agents as is membership in the national community.[15]

Some global advocates are taking steps to solve this problem. For example, in North Carolina it has been proposed that second and third graders have to say the Pledge of Allegiance only once each year; third graders need only paraphrase it. Fifth graders will design an international postage stamp and create their own national flag. Ninth-grade students will write a new constitution for a perfect society.

Irving H. Buchen, when referring to how futurism might work in the classroom, states, "Both history and futurism can be honored by reconvening the first Constitutional Assembly and drafting anew a portion of the Constitution."[16]

Global Education Illegal?

Proposals such as those in North Carolina are actually illegal in many states. Most states outline the duty of teachers to instill patriotism and to assert the dignity of American citizenship. For example, Washington state law declares emphatically:

> It shall be the duty of all teachers to endeavor to impress on the minds of their pupils the principles of morality, truth, justice, temperance, humanity and patriotism; to instruct them in the principles of free government, and to train them up to the true comprehension of the rights, duty and dignity of American citizenship. (RCW Annotated section 28A.67.110)

> Any teacher who fails to teach patriotism and any school director who permits any teacher to teach, knowing that that teacher fails to teach patriotism, is guilty of a misdemeanor. (RCW Annotated section 28A.67.035)

> The flag of the United States shall be displayed at every public school and students must be given an opportunity to salute the flag by repeating the Pledge of Allegiance at the beginning of every school day. (RCW Annotated, section 28A.02.030)

It would seem that with such strong language in many state codes a case could be made that a school district which adopts the practice and tenets of global education is breaking the law. Concerned citizens should research their state code concerning the duties of teachers. Many advocates of global education at the school district level deny that their program slights the teaching of patriotism or national loyalty. But the evidence put forth by global writers themselves clearly indicates the opposite. Notice the semantic sleight of hand used by James Becker in the following statement:

> A first step in achieving a moral empathy on a global scale is the elimination or reduction of three divisive factors. The first of these is poverty. . . . The second factor is ethnicity. . . . Nationalism is the third divisive factor. National loyalty, however, need not have this effect.[17]

I fail to see the difference between nationalism and national loyalty. Webster defines *nationalism* as, "devotion to, or advocacy of, national interests or national unity and independence." The term *devotion* is synonymous with the term *loyalty*. In fact, Webster's comments that *loyalty* connotes the feeling or sentiment, often strong or even enthusiastic, accompanying the sense of allegiance.

Globalists have tried over the years to make *nationalism* a dirty word and suggest as a replacement a *regional* pride like someone might have for his state or city. One of global education's chief goals is to reduce the spirit of patriotism among young people.

Impediments to Global Education

Donald N. Morris, while on the U.S. committee for UNICEF, referred to atheist philosopher Bertrand Russell's recommendation for "proper" global orientation: "As for the early introduction of history with a global and intercultural emphasis, Russell would teach the folly of divisions among races, nations, and creeds."[18]

Many global writers tend to dance around the idea of one world government because society isn't quite ready to accept that notion. But Joyce and Nicholson are more bold. They name two impediments to global education: battles over what ideology to teach and lack of a global government.

Different Ideologies

Notice the arrogance of these writers as they discuss ideological differences. "The first of these is that this particular area of curriculum is tinged with ideological overtones. . . . Ideological strains such as isolationism, jingoism, and chauvinism militate not only against much of what is being taught in global education but even against teaching it at all."[19]

This sets up the two-camp scenario. The global camp is made up of free thinkers and open-minded, modern individuals while the camp with those who disagree with globalism is made up of isolationists, jingoists (extreme nationalists), and chauvinists.

This us/them mentality, with the *thems* obviously being ignorant bigots, is reflected in a memo circulated among those involved with Seattle Public Schools' global program. Regarding the use of the term *global education*, the memo reads:

> ISSUE: The term *Global Education* is an extreme, political hot-potato at this time. The right-wing Christian groups who defeated Senator George Fleming's bill to support International Education programs use *Global Education* as a synonym for atheistic, communistic humanism—out to destroy God, the family, and American society.

> RECOMMENDATION: District personnel must show immediate sensitivity to this semantic/but painfully real fact—if we talk about this project as a global education project it is likely to become a source of intense and long-term opposition from an extremely vocal minority.

Temporarily safe term is—*multicultural/international curriculum development.*

Notice that the people who objected to global education were labeled right-wing: their religious preference was made an issue, their ignorance was implied throughout, and they were labeled a minority interest group. This was one of my early introductions to the global education issue. As a teacher in Seattle, I sat on the committee to introduce globalism into the Seattle school district; a colleague gave me that memo.

Lack of One World Government

Lee Anderson describes a world-centered school called Twenty-First Century High School. In his description of its curriculum, he subtly substitutes the phrase "global society" for the correct phrase, "global government."

They had begun the year by studying about the socio-political organizations characteristic of human history prior to the rise of nation-states. They had looked at hunting and gathering bands, ancient empires, city-states, and various forms of feudal organizations. Attention then turned to the evolution of the nation-state system in Europe and its subsequent diffusion to the rest of the planet. [My guide] told me the class had spent a good deal of time constructing a simulation depicting the structured characteristics of the classical nation-state system and then systematically modifying and changing the model to illustrate the historical innovations that were transforming the classical system into a global society.[20]

To be consistent, Anderson should have said global government rather than global society. The course was tracing sociopolitical organizations—gathering bands, empires, city-states, feudal organizations, and nation-states. The only enforceable way to move from a nation-state to a world-state is by a world government which subjugates nation-states to the world-state.

All globalists see the diminishment of patriotism as an imperative in education. One globalist points out that U.S. history is usually taught in the fifth, eighth, and eleventh grades. This, of course, is too much time spent promoting patriotism, so he suggests:

> After priorities have been set, a critical step . . . is developing and explicitly stating a rationale for their [educators'] decisions and actions [concerning curriculum]. . . . By being explicit in rationale for why and how decisions are to be made, tradition [meaning traditional time spent on U.S. history] may come under question and action may be taken to change it.[21]

If globalists can reduce the amount of time spent teaching U.S. history, they can reduce the strong bonds of affection for our nation among the young.

Rarely will a global educator bluntly call for the U.S. government to relinquish its sovereignty and defer to a world government, but the net effect of their philosophy would reap the same result.

Exactly what would this world order look like? The previous excerpts from global writers give us some idea. Irving H. Buchen gives us a clear glimpse of his idea of a global society in the book *Learning for Tomorrow: The Role of the Future in Education.*

> [T]he concept of individuality and the whole man are not synonymous. The individual man is stirred by independence, autonomy, and self-reliance; the holistic man by interdependence, collectivism, and reliance. . . .
>
> A collectivized individual is multiple rather than singular. If the traditional notion in the West has been one God, one love, one job, one identity, one country, and one planet, the futuristic notion is many gods, many loves, many jobs, many identities, many countries, and many

planets. The collectivized individual may unexpectedly prove more responsive to and cooperative with overt and official planning of aspects of his life.[22]

Again I must ask why American taxpayers are being asked to fund a program that by its own admission must teach that American values are failures, that we must accept a socialistic form of government, and that eventually the U.S. will need to defer to a global government. American education is paid for by Americans who want American values perpetuated, not systematically destroyed.

Globalists are introducing new political ideas with the hope that those ideas will gradually gain acceptance without going through the proper democratic channels. In fact, they have little regard for proper channels. Global educators have appointed themselves the policy generators of the future. Their philosophy and resulting actions are totally out of line with those of the general public; they will suffer the consequences of their arrogance. The general public will one day revolt against such paternalism, and that day will not be pleasant for the establishment in public education. I hope that reasonable people in education will not provoke the American public by continuing down the path of such narrow global education.

PART THREE

THE RELIGION
BEHIND THE MASK

THE NEW AGE AGENDA

*One of the biggest advantages we have as New
Agers is, once the occult, metaphysical and
New Age terminology is removed, we have concepts and techniques that are very acceptable to
the general public. So we can change the names
and demonstrate the power. In so doing, we
open the New Age door to millions who nor-
mally would not be receptive.*

Dick Sutphen[1]

A Christian teacher working in the Wisconsin public
schools recently sent me this note reporting how New
Age globalism is being introduced in her school.

Enclosed is a copy of the handout I received at the last
Special Education staff meeting. The meeting began with
talking about the various types of learners in a classroom.
Then our guest speaker launched into a talk on Global Education and global issues. The lecture soon transitioned
into the subjects of guided imagery and visualization. I
noticed the handouts listed several New Age authors as
recommended reading. The whole thing was really subtle.

The fact that many globalists have a spiritual agenda behind their stated "secular" goals is the most dangerous and damaging aspect of the entire global education movement. If these globalists are able to infuse their ideas into the education system, children will be instructed in occult mysticism. In fact, many teachers are already perverting children's minds with concepts of the occult. Casual observers may immediately think I am referring to the celebration of Halloween in schools or the reading of stories about witchcraft. The occult philosophy that dovetails with globalism is more subtle, and therefore more dangerous, than such obvious Satanism. The term *occult* simply means secret, hidden, beyond normal perceptions, and mystic.

Dr. Robert Muller, under secretary of the United Nations Economic and Social Council, wrote in his book on global education, *New Genesis: Shaping a Global Spirituality*: "Yes, global education must transcend material, scientific, and intellectual achievements and reach deliberately into the moral and spiritual spheres. . . . The real, the great period of human fulfillment on planet Earth is only now about to begin."[2]

That statement in and of itself need not necessarily be a cause for concern. It could be argued that every action arises out of a moral and spiritual frame of reference. The real question here is to what "spiritual sphere" does Dr. Muller refer? He is certainly emphatic about the necessity of a global spirituality for global education. But what kind of spirituality does he mean?

Karma: The Missing Link

Every philosophy and religion rests on certain concepts or beliefs; the occult is no exception. One important concept held by occultists is the law of karma—the belief that action determines fate. A person who lives a virtuous life builds up good karma, while a person committed to wrongdoing builds bad karma. According to occult belief in reincarnation, the circumstances of one's present incarnation are a consequence of karma established in a former life. Each reincarnation should be used for moving closer to "oneness with the Universe." Followers of occult teaching also believe that we are merely focused energies of the entire universe; that our soul continues though our present physical form decays; that we will continue to be reincarnated until we reach complete union with the universe. Muller speaks affectionately of these beliefs when he refers to the former secretary-general and Buddhist monk, U Thant.

> U Thant often spoke of the law of karma. . . . I am grateful to him for having taught me this law. I hope that his message will continue to spread. . . .
>
> To the concept of the noosphere, or sphere of the mind encompassing all humans, we would be well advised to add those of karma spheres, or sphere of good actions, mettasphere, or sphere of love (from the Buddhist concept of metta, or love and kindness towards all living things), animasphere, or sphere of the universal soul. Then humanity could progress and lift itself upwards towards a total communion with God, the universe and eternity.[3]

Muller believes the law of karma is the missing link in his quest for truth.

> For him [U Thant] it was the harmony between the innermost life and the outer life, or the life of the world and the universe . . . the tuning of the inner person with the great mysteries and secrets around him . . . that each of us came from somewhere and was destined to somewhere. . . . His belief in the long-term improvement of humanity through right individual behavior gave me the last missing piece of the puzzle. . . .
>
> Probably one of the most accurate religions in terms of astrophysics is the Hindu religion with its Year of Brahma,

a very long period of hundreds of millions of years, marked by creation, preservation, destruction and again creation, preservation and destruction. . . .

Lastly, there is Christ's message of resurrection. Many people on this planet do not believe in it. But I have lived with a man like U Thant, who constantly held that we were coming from somewhere and that we were going somewhere. . . . He called it the karma, or the law whereby no action is ever lost. . . . We will be resurrected materially in other life forms on this planet and ultimately into atoms of other stars.[4]

The total of Muller's ideas put forth in his book place him squarely in the realm of occult philosophy. Karma, reincarnation, mystic experience, reaching higher states of consciousness, and becoming one with the "Force" of the universe all smack of the occult.

All Is One

Muller also adheres to the Hindu concept of *prana*—the occult concept that all in the universe is energy and thus it is one. Physical matter is really just dense energy and therefore is *maya* or an illusion. Prana is that energy that underlies all life.

I wish scientists would study the "miracle of faith." Much of our social future would benefit from their findings. The Hindus call it *prana*, "the vital." It is indeed a vital principle, the energy, the motor of the upward path of human civilization. . . .

Hindus call our earth Brahma, or God, for they rightly see no difference between our earth and the divine.[5]

Again, the occult idea of oneness with the universe or being one spark from the universal fire is conveyed by Muller. "[T]he universe is made up of endless cosmoses. . . . I am one of those cosmoses, linked with everything in the heavens and on earth. . . . I could seek, know, and feel in myself the entire universe and Godhead, for I was part of them and they were part of me."[6]

Muller combines Eastern mysticism with United Nations utopianism when he states:

> In particular I would agree with the prophecy of that spiritual believer in the United Nations, Sri Chinmoy, when he said: "At the end, world-wide spiritual ecumenism, expressed in new forms of religious cooperation and institutions, would probably be closest to the heart of the resurrected Christ. . . . There is a famous painting and poster which shows Christ knocking at the tall United Nations building, wanting to enter it. I often visualize in my mind another even more accurate painting: that of a United Nations which would be the body of Christ.[7]

World Core Curriculum

As a centerpiece to his 192-page exhortation to the world to adopt occult mysticism, Muller offers a course outline for teaching global education. He would like to see education focus on four main points: (1) our planetary home and place in the universe, (2) the human family, (3) our place in time, and (4) the miracle of individual human life. Though these categories sound secular in content, it should be noted that taken in the context of his book, *The New Genesis*, Dr. Muller's concept of global education is inextricably bound up in Eastern, occult mysticism.

When I read his bizarre ideas, I was startled at his proposal that such occult concepts be taught in public schools; I doubted that reasonable minds would listen to him. After all, everyone is entitled to write what he likes and to express an opinion. The fact that he proposes such ideas does not mean they will be implemented. So I thought.

An article in *Education Week* declared "Educator Proposes a Global 'Core Curriculum.'" The article reported that Dr. Gordon Cawelti "this month urged representatives of other Western nations and Japan to press for the development of a 'world-core curriculum' based on knowledge that will ensure 'peaceful and cooperative existence among the human species on this planet.'" Dr. Cawelti is the executive director of the Association for Supervision and Curriculum Development (ASCD)—an association of education leaders around the nation: superintendents, curriculum directors, administrators, and teachers. Their main organizational objective is to carry on training and proliferate information regarding current curriculum, much of which is worthwhile and important. Its size, approximately 80,000 members, and credible reputation makes the ASCD an influential force in public education.

The article on core curriculum stated, "Mr. Cawelti's world-core curriculum would be based, he said, on proposals put forth by Robert Muller, assistant secretary-general of the United Nations, in his recent book *New Genesis: Shaping a Global Spirituality.*"[8]

Our Planetary Home

The newspaper article quoting Cawelti described each of the four main elements of Muller's program. "Our Planetary Home [includes] studies of the universe, space, the sun, and the earth, with particular attention to the earth's atmosphere, plant and animal life, energy sources, and preserving the ecosystem."[9] But what he didn't point out was that Muller's underlying motivation is to teach children that:

> The scientists have now come to the end of their wisdom. . . . This is where spirituality or religion comes in. Science in my view is part of the spiritual process; it is the transcendence and elevation of the human race into an ever vaster (sic) knowledge and consciousness of the uni-

verse and of its unfathomable, divine character. We can show children and people that there is something divine, miraculous, and tremendous in being human, that God must have a special design for us, that our evolution makes more and more sense, that it will continue at ever higher levels until this planet has finally become a showcase in the universe, a planet of God.[10]

In the context of Muller's overall philosophy, the "higher levels" embody the laws of karma and reincarnation. So, in the context of Muller's overall philosophy, unstated by Cawelti, a study of our planetary home is important for understanding our evolution into higher states of oneness with the universe.

The Human Family

Dr. Cawelti describes Muller's second major element, "The Human Family," as "a review of 'the total world population,' including discussions of human migration, geography, races, sexes, children, health, living standards, and social organizations."[11] But Cawelti did not mention that Muller concludes this section by stating:

> The supreme reality of the human family, universal and interdependent, as seen by Christ and by all great religious leaders must now become the world's major political objective. The time has come for the implementation of a spiritual vision of world affairs. The entire planet must elevate itself again into the spiritual, cosmic throbbing of the universe.[12]

The idea that the whole human race must participate in "higher states of consciousness" is a basic element of occult preparation for a new world. Astrologer and author of *Occult Preparations for a New Age,* Dane Rudhyar states that, "the initial manifestation, public and collective, of such an exalted state of consciousness demands the formation of a planetary type of society. The possibility of it is now with us."[13]

As though writing in duet with Rudhyar, Muller refers to the role of karma in the development of planetary consciousness: "What a formidable force it will be when all 4.5 billion humans on this planet have become spiritual beings in the eternal stream of time, conscious of the long-term consequences of their lives and actions."[14]

Teaching children of the human family is, according to Muller, more than just geography and social studies; it is a movement toward oneness with the universe.

Our Place in Time

Dr. Cawelti watered down what Muller said about the third element of his global education program, "Our Place in Time." Cawelti simply stated that this referred to "courses that would help students understand the history of the planet and of 'human institutions,' with the goal of learning about 'mistakes that have been made and can be avoided.'"[15] But in Muller's fully developed concept, he includes the above statement about 4.5 billion people becoming spiritual beings and fulfilling their karma. In his section on our place in time, Muller also states that ultimately children should learn that they are

> universal beings ready to flower and to fulfill their divine lives or cosmic destinies. . . . In us humans there are divine cosmic elements which will flower to the point that we will become conscious of the total universe and that the universe will become conscious in ourselves. . . . The incarnated God, or Christ, is in all of us and for all of us to manifest.[16]

The idea that we are all gods and that we can attain a Christ consciousness is central to occult mysticism.

The Miracle of Individual Life

In describing the fourth and final element of Muller's global education, the article on Cawelti's core curriculum states that the "Miracle of Individual Life" would entail "studies that would provide students with the knowledge necessary to develop 'good physical, mental, moral, and spiritual lives.'"[17]

But Muller describes it somewhat differently. "It is becoming increasingly clear in our debates on human rights that the individual is the alpha and the omega of all our efforts. Individual human life is the highest form of universal or divine consciousness on our planet."[18]

Certainly that is one religious opinion, but it should not be taught in public schools under the guise of global education.

When discussing what "good spiritual life" means, he defers to the Buddhist monk U Thant for an explanation. He states that good spiritual life means "spiritual exercises of interiority, meditation, prayer and communion with God, the universe and eternity."[19]

Some Christians might find that statement acceptable because of his reference to prayer and communion with God. Actually his statement reveals more about his occult leanings than it does about a familiarity with true Christianity. How does one commune with the universe and eternity? This is not a Christian, but an occult thought.

Muller concludes his outline of what he sees as the ultimate goal of global education: "The unique challenge to universal spiritual education is to integrate our vast scientific knowledge, our social knowledge, our knowledge of time and of the art of living into a shining, divine, blissful vision of our miraculous journey in the unfathomable universe."[20]

His idea of our journey in the fathomless universe is more clearly tied to his push for global education when he writes what the Earth might say if it could talk:

After your cave age, after your tribal age, after your feudal age, after your national age, you have at long last entered *my* age, the global age. But this is still insufficient, for you have yet to enter the cosmic or divine age and see your proper place in the fathomless universe and time. You still have to become the planet of God.[21]

Muller's global education, endorsed by ASCD, is but a step toward a completely new age in human history. He sees global education as a means to a spiritual, utopian society. Muller clearly states this as his final goal when he says: "I have come to believe firmly today that our future peace, justice, fulfillment, happiness and harmony on this planet will not depend on world government but on divine or cosmic government."[22]

After mankind has reached this new age, this cosmic or divine age, Muller writes that God will look down on us and say: "I will now make My peace with you and let you establish a perfect Earth. Farewell, my grown-up children. At long last, you are on the right path, you have brought heaven down to earth and found your proper place in the universe."[23]

Once a school district accepts global education that deals with economics, politics, and technology, it will after a few years be ready to "reach beyond" those things and delve more fully into occult spheres. By then this will seem like a natural transition. After all, when people discuss topics of international peace and cooperation, which in themselves are not harmful, the question of how to achieve a better world will continually come up and at the root of the discussion will lie the spiritual dimension. This is when occult teachings will be accepted and presented by those already teaching materialistic globalism. Such teaching uses pseudoscientific language to mask its religious nature, making it seem like the next logical step in progressive, secular education.

Psychic Fairs and Globalism

While living in Seattle, I read in the paper that there was to be a fair on ESP, physic phenomena, Tarot card reading, aura readings, and dozens of occult practices. By this time in my research, I had a sneaking suspicion that the fair might also contain information on global education. I was right. In the middle of a large room filled with booths selling occult books, meditation tapes, people who would photograph your aura, psychic healers, mind readers and palm readers, I found a display from The World University Development Association (WUDA) promoting "Implementing a Global Plan for the Future of Education and World Peace." Had I not already read Muller's book on occult global education, I would have thought this display out of place. Actually, it was right at home.

The WUDA literature used the usual global education jargon; to the casual observer (outside this particular setting), the WUDA would have seemed like any other global education clearinghouse. The materials made occasional references to the need for spiritual unity, but this seems like a noble thought these days—a nicety like saying babies are cute. I asked the man at the booth, who was the founder of the association, if current global education which merely focused on politics and economics was moving in the wrong direction. His response was most revealing. He said that the current direction of global education was good. "You work with whatever they can relate to," he said, "like peace. You start there, but then you ask 'how do we achieve peace?'" Motioning toward the room buzzing with occult activities, he responded to his own question, "That's where all this comes in."[24]

The School of Ageless Wisdom

Besides the occult concepts reflected in Muller's book on global education, there is his connection with the School of

Ageless Wisdom in Arlington, Texas—a private school which seeks to infuse occult philosophy into its curriculum. In a telephone interview, Dr. Muller insisted that he had "no affiliation with such esoteric writings or groups." He clarified that "if they find some association with what I have said, that is fine, but I do not ascribe to their teachings." However, he did lend them his name for use in promoting their curriculum and was in full knowledge of their occult teachings. In fact, by his own admission, he addresses an "esoteric group" each year. The School of Ageless Wisdom recently developed a global education school and curriculum, and with Muller's blessing, called it "The World Core Curriculum in the Robert Muller School."

The fact is that Muller's philosophy so closely aligns with occult teaching that although he may not overtly associate with "such esoteric groups," *they* find no problem accepting what *he* teaches.

In the preface to the program, the authors state that "the underlying philosophy upon which the Robert Muller School is based will be found in the teachings set forth in the books of Alice A. Bailey by the Tibetan teacher, Djwhal Khul."[25] Alice A. Bailey's works can be found in any occult bookstore. She was a major channel for "the Masters"[26]— spiritual gurus—to telepathically transfer their message from Tibet to the West. Known as "the Messenger of the Masters" and a Master himself, Djwhal Khul is a major focal point for demonic spirits to transfer their message to the world of human beings.

Alice Bailey's books chart the spirit hierarchy emanating from Sanat Kumara, Lord of the World, a spirit being who came to earth eleven million years ago. This is all very bizarre, to say the least. It doesn't matter whether you believe *what* these occult writers say; it only matters that you understand that they are saying it and that men like Muller find common ground with them. And that men like Dr.

Cawelti endorse men like Dr. Muller. And that your public school may someday use something from this religion, though by then it will be watered down and more palatable.

After my phone conversation with Dr. Muller, he sent me the *Evaluation Report of the ROBERT MULLER SCHOOL for the SOUTHERN ASSOCIATION OF COLLEGES AND SCHOOLS (SACS)*. This report is an evaluation for accreditation. The evaluators, made up of college professors, wrote the following recommendation.

> The visiting team from the Southern Association were so impressed with the program being offered at the Robert Muller School that they thought the educational process and the general curriculum would be most valuable as a model for teacher education.
>
> [The school believes] that a global curriculum is essential to meet the needs of a rapidly changing society and the interconnectedness of the global community. The most current educational processes recommended by the most advanced research on brain-mind and human development are being used to enhance the mental, physical and spiritual development of each child.
>
> The school should strive to provide educators everywhere information about the curriculum and methodologies used at the Robert Muller School.
>
> The greater the visibility of these children in their student activities, the greater the potential for sharing this type of educational experience with others. The Robert Muller School model of student activities is already being shared with many, but it is recommended that a continued effort be carried out in this vein.
>
> The Robert Muller School is an exceptional model in our contemporary world. . . . Many public school systems are too limited by institutional constraints to provide the type of education offered at this school. However, throughout this report the committee has recommended that information of the school's educational processes be shared with educators everywhere as much as possible. . . .

[T]he committee believes strongly that many more parents would be committed to their children's education, if they saw them receiving the learning and development opportunities that the children in the Robert Muller School are receiving.

A television series with accompanying study guide and reading material should be produced, if at all possible, to disseminate this model.[27]

Not only did the committee recommend accreditation for this occult school, but they encourage "educators everywhere" to use the occult practices. With such an enthusiastic response in the education community, you should be concerned that it soon may come knocking at your school district's door.

Dr. Muller is not alone in his desire for a new age, or a divine and cosmic age which only uses the global education movement as a means to a spiritual end. The Association for Supervision and Curriculum Development has already built a strong bridge between Muller's occult teachings and its implementation into public schools. But the philosophy he champions is held by thousands already infusing their occult mysticism into classrooms.

NEW AGERS
IN PUBLIC SCHOOLS

There shall not be found among you any one
that maketh his son or his daughter to pass
through the fire, or that useth divination, or an
observer of times, or an enchanter, or a witch.
Or a charmer, or a consulter with familiar spir-
its, or a wizard, or a necromancer. For all who
do these things are an abomination to the LORD.

Deuteronomy 18:10–12

A classic example of the kind of masquerade occurring in public schools was illustrated in an elementary school in the Los Angeles, California, area.

Groups of five second graders were taken from their classes each week and run through lessons on guided imagery and self-hypnosis. This was part of a program called "Developing Understanding of Self and Others." The children were in the program for six weeks before the parents found out about it. Parents who contacted me due to this program were especially concerned because some of their children had difficulty even remembering what occurred during the covert sessions.

After numerous complaints from parents, the school administration announced that the program was to be dropped and a more acceptable self-esteem program was to be installed. But later, when questioned about the new programs' activity, the children explained that they were doing almost exactly the same guided imagery and self-hypnosis. This time, however, the children also shared with their parents that the counselor had told them to keep the sessions secret. When questioned by the parents, the children's teacher revealed that she didn't know what the counseling sessions involved.

In another program a Connecticut teacher received "Celebration of Excellence" recognition for teaching children in first through fourth grade to "reduce stress." His method? He teaches children progressive muscle relaxation, deep breathing exercises, visualization techniques, and biofeedback. This sounds harmless, but the techniques parallel more blatantly labeled New Age rituals.

A program used in Indiana called "Tactics for Thinking" supposedly teaches thinking skills to children. Many of the exercises are fine; however, also included are "memory enhancing" techniques that teach children guided imagery. The technique parallels New Age methods for inducing out-of-the-body experiences.

Spiritual global education goes beyond political/economic global education. The latter is only a means to the former. However, not all global educators hold to such spiritual ideas. Spiritual globalism is the goal primarily of those in the occult/New Age movement. They emphasize that we are at the "dawning of the age of Aquarius;" we are in preparation for a new age and a new culture. In fact, Muller states emphatically, "Humanity is ready for a new culture."[1]

While New Age disciples constantly mask their true intent by using "scientific" terms, astrologer Dane Rudhyar outlines their whole agenda in his straightforward book, *Occult Preparations for a New Age.* At least he is honest; those preparing for the "new age" are heavily into the occult. To recognize what is happening in society today, we must change our image of the occult. Most people immediately think of movies like *The Exorcist* or ghoulish demons and witches dressed in black. The occult of today is a complex and sophisticated religion that promises love, joy, peace, long-suffering, and fulfillment. It supposedly loves light and seeks to bring out the best in people. Closely aligned with Eastern mysticism, the occult believes in the reincarnation of the soul until the soul joins in perfect communion with the universe.

The one central theme of the New Age movement is radical, mystical transformation on a personal level. This transformation, New Age globalists hope, will eventually spread out and bring about planetary peace and prosperity. Humankind will be unified, possessing a common religion and common ideals.

Leading New Age activist Dick Sutphen outlines the four central doctrines of New Age theology:

1. All Is One: The external world and consciousness are one and the same.

2. Man Is a Divine Being: We are all part of God, so we are God.

3. Life Is for Evolutionary Purposes: Karma and reincarnation.

4. Self-Actualization: Awareness of the true self within leads to mastery of your own reality.[2]

But how does all this relate to global education? New Agers believe that for the world to enter the New Age, it must have a planetary consciousness. In order to do this, we must begin to think globally. Basically they are using political/economic global education to someday reach spiritual global consciousness. This transition will be a gradual one. Even now, threads of New Age spirituality are being woven into the public school fabric. A few years from now the currently watered-down New Age concepts will be accepted in full. The constant quest for innovation makes education vulnerable to more innovative teaching methods and content of the New Age type. And as the proverbial frog slowly boils in the water gradually heated, so the education establishment will accept New Age occultism as standard, even essential, education.

Transformation and Teachers

New Age occultism is beginning to crop up in public education. Marilyn Ferguson states that of the New Agers surveyed:

> More were involved in education than in any other single category of work. They were teachers, administrators, policy makers, educational psychologists. . . . Subtle forces are at work, factors you are not likely to see in banner headlines. For example, tens of thousands of classroom teachers, educational consultants and psychologists, counselors, administrators, researchers, and faculty members in colleges of education have been among the millions engaged in *personal transformation.* (emphasis added)[3]

Under the guise of psychology and inner unfoldment, occult thinking is infiltrating many institutions. Ferguson further explains that these "Aquarian conspirators" are being aided by "scientific research." She comments that: "Research in brain function and consciousness demonstrates that teaching must change if we are to tap our potential."[4]

Canadian psychologist Herbert Koplowitz's advanced level of cognitive development, which he calls Unitary Operational Thought, reflects such "scientific" ideas. This sounds very scientific and intimidating until it is explained that Unitary Operational Thought is an understanding that "the way we perceive the external world is only one of many possible constructs."[5] This is basic Eastern mysticism which states that all is energy, and thus the external world is an illusion based upon our own perception. Koplowitz admits that "mystic traditions such as Taoism may offer one of the most thoroughly developed bodies of Unitary Operational Thought."[6] But, of course, if he asked people to convert to Taoism to begin with, he wouldn't get too far in the Western world.

Altered States of Consciousness

One New Age pseudoscience is transpersonal education, described as education to teach the whole person and help students find themselves. Ferguson claims that it is "imbedded in sound science," but the activities she describes are merely occult exercises. Transpersonal education involves what she calls an understanding of mind and body integration which is, in reality, a fancy name for yoga or meditation. She reveals that it relies heavily on the use of altered and expanded consciousness. This, again, is merely occultism—reaching the higher self, becoming one with the universe, projecting into the astral plane. Ferguson points out that transpersonal psychology springs from the "world's spiritual disciplines."[7] One New Age educator remarks, "Transpersonal education is the process of exposing people to the mysterious in themselves."[8] In 1979, Ferguson observed, "The deliberate use of consciousness-expanding techniques in education, only recently well under way, is new in mass schooling."[9] These techniques are no longer new in many schools. She further reveals that, "Because of its power for social healing and awakening, they [New Age educators] conspire to bring the philosophy into the class-room, in every grade."[10]

Consciousness-expanding techniques include anything that deals with enhancing the "inner experience, such as centering exercises, guided imagery, dream journals, pre-cognition, and creative visualization (the occult version).

Meditation in Class

An example of the use of occultism in the classroom is seen in the use of centering exercises. *Centering* is just another name for meditation or watered-down yoga. Two books that will help you understand it are *The Centering Book: Awareness Activities for Children, Parents, and Teachers* and *The Second Centering Book,* both by Gay Hendricks and Thomas B. Roberts. The subjects covered in these books include relaxing the mind, working with dreams, guided imagery, sufi stories, intuition activities, energizing exercises, and ESP activities. In the bibliography of their second volume, the authors list nineteen books or articles on transcendental meditation (TM) for further understanding of center-ing.[11] However, in 1976, a federal district court declared TM a religion, and as such, illegal to practice in public schools.

Their bibliography also includes Alice A. Bailey's *Education in the New Age.* The authors even comment that: "A few years ago biofeedback, meditation, yoga, relaxation, guided imagery, and brain hemisphere specialization were on the fringes of education. . . . Now, thanks to the people whose writings (and other media) appear here, a new door has opened to help us reach traditional goals and even go be-yond them to new kinds of learning, to new ways of teach-ing, and to higher objectives."[12]

New Age disciples Jack Canfield and Paula Klimek wrote in *New Age* magazine that, "Centering can also be ex-tended into work with meditation in the classroom. (Advice: If you're teaching in a public school, don't call it meditation, call it 'centering.' Every school wants children to be relaxed, attentive and creative, and that's what they will get.)"[13]

This attempt at deceiving public school officials is explained by Dane Rudhyar in his book *Occult Preparation for a New Age.* He reveals that occult terminology most likely will not be used when publicly describing occult activity.

> In order gradually to convince the old guard of official thinkers in control of most social and educational processes . . . they feel obliged to compromise and tone down their direct . . . realizations by using indirect techniques. . . . References to metaphysical principles unfamiliar to the European tradition are avoided.[14]

Guided Imagery and Visualization

Guided imagery and creative visualization are two other methods New Age globalists use to prepare children for a planetary consciousness. Don't be confused by the terminology. Everyone uses their imagination to be creative and anyone listening to a story is engaged in guided imagery to some degree. Guided imagery and creative visualization of the New Age sort go far beyond these harmless practices.

Guided imagery and visualization exercises vary in content but have common characteristics. The children must sit or lie still with their eyes closed. They relax each muscle of the body. They lower their rate of breathing. Finally, they create mental images of scenes described by the teacher and mentally transport themselves into those scenes.

The Association of Supervision and Curriculum Development created a program called "Tactics for Thinking." This program has children go through "deep processing" in which they are to follow the standard guided imagery practices while thinking of historical figures—picture George Washington on his horse; smell the leather of his saddle; or, before writing about snow, picture yourself as a snowflake falling through the sky.

The teacher is instructed in the manual to use a warm-up exercise by having students practice creating images. The manual suggests the students imagine a blue ball hovering in space. The teacher is to make the exercise more complex by adding other objects such as colored squares.

This particular exercise is alarmingly similar to rituals used to induce out of the body experiences. D. Scott Rogo, in his book *Leaving The Body: A Complete Guide to Astral Projection*, lists as the first step in astral projection to, "develop the ability to activate the imagination." He suggests beginning with certain occult symbols such as a blue circle. He emphasizes that, "most of these occult teachings advise the student to develop intense imagery skills before using visualization for actually leaving the body."[15] Rogo points out that the primary application of teaching people these techniques is to reduce their fear of death by having them experience the realm of spirits. If my spirit can reach into the spiritual world and see that reincarnation is waiting for me on the other side of death, there certainly is no need for salvation through Christ.

Shakti Gawain, in her book *Creative Visualization*, writes:

> Creative visualization is not just a technique, but ultimately a state of consciousness. It is a consciousness in which we deeply realize that we are the continuous creators of our universe and we take responsibility for that at all moments.
>
> There is no separation between us and God. . . . Creative visualization is the process of realizing and making visible on the physical plane our divine potential.[16]

Teaching Children to Talk to the Spirits

Dr. Beverly Galyean was a Los Angeles public schools' consultant for a program called "confluent education." In her book *Language from Within,* she suggests that children in all grades, including kindergarten, be led into "guided fantasies." But listen to the type of trip she offers.

> Close your eyes and relax, I will lead you in a guided fantasy. Imagine . . . a very beautiful valley. . . . Ahead of you is a mountain. . . . You have magic powers so climbing . . . is easy. . . . at the top . . . look into the sun and as you do the face of a very wise person slowly appears. You . . . ask . . . "What must I do to find happiness in my life right now?" The person answers. . . . Listen to this person speaking. . . . You may . . . engage in a conversation. When you feel finished with your conversation, come back to us here in the room. Write an account of what was spoken between you and the wise person.[17]

In a lecture at a New Age conference called the Mandala Conference (Hindus use a mandala to symbolize the power of the gods, and it is a vehicle for meditation), Galyean said that "many schools are quite open to overtly religious technologies such as meditation. In more conservative areas, it is necessary to use euphemistic terms such as *centering* and *focusing* to describe meditation."[18]

Again, deception is used to mask the real intent. At the Confluent Education Workshop in the Mandala Conference in San Diego on August 4, 1980, Galyean demonstrated the technique of guided imagery used in her program. She related that the teacher tells children to see themselves full of light. They are to "image" themselves containing all the light of the universe. With that light the children will then feel at peace—they are perfect, she claims.

This idea of being filled with the light of the universe is exactly the same as the concept described by occult writers Melita Denning and Osborne Phillips in their book, Creative Visualization. Both Denning and Phillips hold high grades of initiation in the occult society, the Qabalistic Order Aurum Solis.

Some educators may think that conjuring up pictures of yourself as perfect and focusing on your Higher Self is just a good example of positive thinking and promoting self-esteem. Some might say that what Galyean is teaching in public schools and what occult writers like Denning and Osborne teach are radically different. The evidence indicates that at best Galyean's program is only more palatable. The occult concepts are identical.

The real danger is that children are being prepared to become more involved in occult activity. Denning and Osborne point out that while practicing creative visualization from their book for such positive things as self-esteem and attaining greater success,

> you are also being given different parts of a Way of Life which is recognized, and has been recognized by teachers of Wisdom in different cultures and ages. . . . As you proceed further and further in the development of your inner powers, you should gradually become more aware of the existence of the living reality of your Higher Self.[19]

The Higher Self is not to be confused with noble character. In both occult and New Age thinking, the Higher Self is another name for the realm of God. Denning and Osborne comment that the "World of the Divine . . ." is the place "in which the Higher Self functions."[20]

Galyean explains the basis for confluent education.

> Once we begin to see that we are all God, that we all have the attributes of God, then I think the whole purpose of human life is to reown the Godlikeness within us; the perfect love, the perfect wisdom, the perfect understanding, the perfect intelligence, and when we do that we create back to that old, that essential oneness which is consciousness. So my whole view is very much based on that idea.[21]

It is startling that such occult ideas are being taught in public schools, but what is really alarming is that Galyean's program and others like it are actually introducing children to "spirit guides." New Agers involved with contacting spirit guides believe that guides are essential for ushering in the new age of global consciousness. Shakti Gawain, in her book *Creative Visualization*, devotes a chapter to meeting your spirit guide. After a person achieves a meditative state, he is to look for a "being." "Greet this being," she writes. "Ask your guide if there is anything he or she would like to say to you, or any advice to give you at the moment."[22] Gawain's book appears in several bibliographies for guided imagery programs used in public schools.

When explaining how first graders in public schools are introduced to their own special being from the spirit world, Beverly Galyean remarks, "Of course we don't call them that in public schools. We call them imaginary guides."[23] New Agers like Galyean, however, believe these guides are real, not imaginary.

Occult writer Ruth Montgomery gives us a clear picture of how "the guides" operate. She has written many books "automatically." After spending the morning in meditation, she places her fingers on the keys of her typewriter, and the guides type answers to her questions. In her book, *Strangers Among Us*, she quotes the guides explaining to her how they work. She writes, "We in this dimension are working regularly with those who have learned to raise their vibratory levels to a frequency where we are able to lower ours, and meld the thoughts."[24]

Raising the vibratory level is a reference to reaching into the Higher Self. Remember, occultism sees everything as energy and thus, communication with spirits is done through proper energy "vibrations."

In their book, *Beyond Biofeedback*, leading biofeedback practitioners Elmer and Alyce Green wrote about the dangers of spirit guides. They commented that, "a woman wrote that after her husband had taken the [mind training] course, one of his 'imaginary psychic advisors' unexpectedly began speaking to him without being asked."[25]

Under the guise of humanistic education—meaning humane approaches to education—teachers are involved in occult practices in one form or another in classrooms all across the country. Marilyn Ferguson quotes Galyean describing the methods of infusing such practices into the traditional curriculum:

> Around Los Angeles hundreds of people are practicing this kind of education, but fear permeates the environment because of a call for "fundamentals," discipline, control. . . . The individual humanistic teacher, counselor, administrator, parent, or student is left wondering how to merge a philosophy of love, openness, trust, belief in process and learning from within, creative expression, personal responsibility, and group consensus with a tradition that seems its opposite.
>
> Our answer: Take the need where it is. Provide creative alternatives to those programs that no longer work. If your district wants "back to basics," improved reading scores, and better attendance, show them how your humanistic program, or the program of your colleagues, accomplishes these goals. You can use traditional subject matter to provide students with processes for self-reflection.
>
> Or, if your district wants discipline, tell them about programs that operate on the principle of internal control. . . . Perhaps hyperactivity is a problem at your school. Use natural methods for calming over-active energies: yoga, meditation, massage, movement, nutrition. No one can learn when the environment is distracting, fragmented. Learn how to lead focusing activities, group meditations, and relaxing techniques. . . .
>
> The crises now facing most school districts can be the springboard for your own humanistic experiments.[26]

Recently, the Los Angeles public schools took Galyean's recommendation and launched a program that introduces children to mystic trances, contacting spirit guides, and even conjuring up the dead.

HYPNOTIZING CHILDREN INTO THE OCCULT

For he said unto him, Come out of the man,
thou unclean spirit. And he asked him, What is
thy name? And he answered saying, My name
is Legion: for we are many.

Mark 5:8–9

The plainly wrapped brown package arrived just a day before he phoned our offices at Citizens for Excellence in Education. "Did you get the curriculum material I sent?" he asked. "It's a terrible program," he continued. "Just terrible. You must try to stop it." He wouldn't reveal his name for fear of jeopardizing his teaching position in the Los Angeles school district.

Frankly, I hadn't looked at the material he had sent. I opened the package and found the typed pages of a pilot curriculum used in the Los Angeles public schools called Mission S.O.A.R. As I read through the program, I was shocked at what I found.

Mission S.O.A.R.—Set Objectives, Achieve Results—starts in the third grade, and on the surface it sounds wonderful. It purports to solve a crisis now facing the district: gang violence. The program's director claims that this non-traditional approach can be used as a self-esteem program, a program to enhance a drug and alcohol curriculum, a supplement to sex education, as well as an approach to curbing gang violence. It also will supposedly increase children's academic achievement.

It *may* do all that. Its results would be difficult to measure. What it definitely *does* is introduce children to their own personal spirit guide and teach them to conjure up the dead.

Early in the program's lesson is a session called "Rainbow for Relaxation." Its stated objective is to help the children relax. The actual activity is hypnosis. The teacher is instructed to say to the class: "Have you ever felt so nervous that your body shook? Have you ever been so grumpy that your friends turned away? Have you ever been too tired to do your schoolwork? I'm going to show you a safe and healthy way of controlling your shaking body, grumpy attitude, and tired body. You will feel more energy, happiness, and serenity. The more you practice this method, the better you'll get with it."[1]

The children are instructed to sit up straight and close their eyes while the teacher keeps the window blinds open and turns out the lights. The teacher then reads a three-page script to the children. The script describes a guided journey to Hawaii. Once on the beach the children are told to look up and see a beautiful rainbow.

> This rainbow is so gorgeous that you decide to settle down under a palm tree to relax and just gaze at it for a while.
>
> By looking carefully at the colors in the rainbow, you notice that the first color at the top of the rainbow is red.

See the color red and feel your whole body, all the parts of your body, go limp and completely relax. . . . The next color you see is orange. . . . Notice your feelings because we are going to think of orange as your feelings color. . . . Move on down the rainbow to yellow. As you see the color yellow, feel your thoughts and mind growing calm and peaceful. . . . From now on, whenever you see the color yellow, you will calm and rest your mind. . . . Continue down the rainbow to the color green. . . . From now on, whenever you see the color green, allow peace to fill your life. . . . Move down the rainbow to blue. . . . You are now able to be loving and kind. . . . From now on, whenever you see the color blue, feel yourself full of love. . . . Move on down the rainbow and see the color purple . . . begin to know the *real* you. Feel calm. . . . Move down the rainbow and see the color violet. . . . Enter this *real* part of you. From now on, whenever you see the color violet, be at your rainbow and use it for any good purpose you want.

While in this hypnotic state, the children are told to repeat to themselves, "I like myself; I am happy; I am in perfect health; I have full control of myself; I am using more and more of my mind each day. Everyday, in every way, I am growing better, better, better."

The children are brought out of the trance with the message: "Don't do it yet, but in a few minutes you will return from the rainbow by seeing in your mind the colors of the rainbow in reverse order, from violet to red. On reaching red, your eyes will be open, and you will be wide awake, healthy, full of energy, refreshed and in tune with life."

It is a sad commentary on society when we feel we have reached the desperate point of having to hypnotize young people into good behavior and healthy attitudes. I hardly think that parents send their children to school to undergo such treatment.

Developing Your Psychic Power

This blatant hypnosis of children is shocking. Yet even more disturbing is the close parallel to exercises outlined in the book *Beyond Hypnosis: A Program for Developing Your Psychic and Healing Power*, by leading psychic William W. Hewitt. Hewitt also uses the seven colors of the rainbow to bring his students into an hypnotic state. However, he reveals that "in this session you took a significant step toward reaching your level of psychic functioning."[2]

The "feelings" the children are to associate with each color described in Mission S.O.A.R. are identical to the supposed *chakras* in the body. Chakras—or energy sources—are taught by New Agers to be located along the spine and are supposedly important in the use of meditation and psychic powers. All of this in itself is appalling. But this particular program gets worse.

Conjuring Up the Dead and Spirit Guides

The next lesson for the school children after "Rainbow for Relaxation" is called "Workshop and Helpers." The stated objective is to create the ideal environment for problem solving and creative thinking.

The teacher is instructed to introduce the lesson with this message: "How would you like a special or custom-built house to go to anytime you want to, with anything you want in it? You could have any person you want to come and visit you. It wouldn't matter if he or she was dead or alive, real or imaginary. After today, you will always have this special place and special way of being with anyone you want. Be sure to use them."

Necromancy—attempting to contact the dead through sorcery—is a serious abomination before the Lord. In Deuteronomy, chapter 18, God specifically refers to the sin of spiritism, witchcraft, and necromancy. The children in this program are encouraged to pursue it and pursue it regularly.

Hewitt teaches the exact same procedure. He instructs his students to create a "psychic workshop for all your psychic work."[3] He also introduces the importance of conjuring up the dead by using the workshop. He points out in one of his lessons that, "in this session you will experience communication with a deceased person. Deceased persons can be a source of valuable information for you."[4]

The teacher leads the children through the hypnotic rainbow exercise and has them visualize building their workshop. When this is done, the children are told:

> Now sit down in your big chair behind your table and relax. Get ready to meet your two helpers. . . . First, you will see your male helper. He is behind the sliding door in your elevator. Use the control panel on the arm of your chair to make the door of your elevator open. . . . Now, look at your male helper. . . . He is now real and alive, and he comes into your workshop. . . . say "Hello" and ask him his name. . . . tell him how glad you are that he is there with you. . . . Ask him either to sit or stand near you on your right side.

The same procedure is used to introduce the children's female helper. Notice that the children are to ask the spirit guides' names rather than use their imagination to give them a name. This is certainly not just a child's imagination being used; this is true demonic contact.

In almost an exact parallel, occult leader William Hewitt tells his readers:

> In this session you will meet your two advisors. . . . Now press the control button [on your chair] to open the door into your workshop. Now mentally say, "I welcome my male advisor into my workshop. Please enter and sit in your chair." . . . Greet your male advisor. Ask him his name. Study his appearance. Thank him for coming. . . .

Now, mentally say, "I welcome my female advisor into my workshop."[5]

In a blasphemous parallel to the ever-present comfort of the Holy Spirit, the child in the public school program is told, "Know that he will always be there on your right side whenever you need him." The same is said of the female helper introduced to each child.

Once introduced to the two helpers, the children are told to show acceptance of the spirits by being sure to, "thank your helpers for being with you and tell them that you look forward to being with them again the next time you enter your workshop. Your helpers are both experts and can help you, teach you, guide you, listen to you and counsel you at any time."

In a footnote to the teacher, the program instructs to "let the students know that they may return to their workshops anytime to help them solve problems."

This is critical thinking skills? This is what secular educators call good education? How can they be blind to the explicit spiritual nature of this lesson? This would be laughable if it were not so tragically dangerous to children.

Setting Goals with Demonic Assistance

Shortly after being introduced to their personal spirit guides, the children learn how to seek the spirits' guidance in setting goals.

In a lesson entitled "New Year's Resolution—Any Time of the Year," the children are taken into their "workshop" by means of the rainbow hypnotic exercise. Once in that state, they are to seek the counsel of their guides. "Today we are going to shop for goals with your imagination. . . . Ask your helpers what would be the best goal for you to choose. Listen to them and then decide what your goal is."

In the psychic book *Beyond Hypnosis*, occult students are told to order their lives in the same way. "Ask your Masters. I probably use this method more often than all other methods combined. Sometimes my Masters solve the problems for me. Other times they give me directions on how to solve the problems for myself."[6]

Think of the generation of children who will grow to adulthood relying on demonic counsel for their decision-making process. These children will be our future judges, legislators, mayors, governors, and presidents. It is incumbent upon all people, including parents who homeschool or send their children to private school, to work to change this dangerous trend in public education.

The children's curriculum in Mission S.O.A.R. tells the children: "As you leave your workshop, stand for a moment under the bright, white light which has been installed over your door. Feel its warmth throughout your entire body."

Compare that with what Hewitt tells his occult pupils:

This is your pure psychic light which comprises all frequencies and fills you with ability to perform as a psychic for any worthwhile purpose. Stand a moment and allow the light to go in through every pore in your skin, filling you completely. You are filled with light. You are clear and radiant. You are filled with psychic power.[7]

Tragically children have received little solid instruction in how to make good decisions. In the 1970s and 1980s, children were taught decision-making skills through a method known as *values clarification*—a method based on self-interest rather than a moral Right that transcended one's personal whims and circumstances. More and more educators are now seeing that values clarification was a failure. Unfortunately, a growing number of educators' "better alternative" is to teach demonic contact for decision-making counsel.

Parents are currently working to have these portions of Mission: S.O.A.R. removed. Even if they are successful, it is doubtful that New Age educators will cease to press for the infusion of the occult into curriculum.

What could be in store for children involved in Mission S.O.A.R.? Psychic leader William Hewitt, like the school program, moves his students from the hypnotic rainbow lesson to meeting two spirit guides. But he goes beyond that. He teaches his pupils to make contact with either a highly powerful demon or Lucifer himself—the angel of light.

> In a moment, I will ask you to push your control button. When you push it, the door will open and the Master of All Masters will enter and proceed directly to you. The Master of All Masters will encompass you and impress on you . . . what you are to do with your life. No one but you will know the message the Master of All Masters gives you. . . . [He] enters, bathed in the most brilliant light you have ever seen [he gives his message]. . . . You have your personal charter. . . . Your guests [other spirits] are gone. But you are not alone because you have them all as part of you now . . . forever.[8]

Intuition—Entrance to the Spirit World

The latest trend in education is whole brain learning. A lot of "scientific" jargon is thrown around about left brain/right brain research, but what New Agers believe is that traditional education focuses too much on the analytical side of the brain and not enough on the affective side of the brain. They claim the affective hemisphere of the brain deals with things like creativity and intuition. What is needed, they say, is to join the two aspects of the brain and have holistic education that teaches the whole brain.

I am not refuting the major findings of brain research, nor am I refuting many of the ideas of a more humane and individualized education. But how is whole brain learning achieved? Ferguson writes, "Meditation, chanting, and similar techniques increase the coherence and harmony in the brain wave patterns," and, "Incantations, mantras, poetry, and secret sacred words are all bridges that join the two brains."[9] Secret sacred words? Again, New Age educators see occult activity as *the* ultimate in good education. But New Agers go beyond occult activities and move into occult encounters.

Those who emphasize whole brain learning often talk of the use of intuition as a nonanalytical way of knowing. They claim that using intuition will boost creativity and help achieve the goals of traditional education. Ferguson writes, "The scientific validation of 'intuition,' our term for knowing that can't be tracked, has shaken science and is just now having its impact on education."[10] She explains that intuition is enhanced by occult means:

> Altered states of consciousness are taken seriously: centering exercises, meditation, relaxation, and fantasy are used to keep the intuitive pathways open and the whole brain learning. Students are encouraged to 'tune in,' imagine, identify the special feeling of peak experiences. There are techniques to encourage body awareness: breathing, relaxation, yoga, movement, biofeedback.[11]

She endorses the use of consciousness-altering techniques because they enhance the whole brain by shifting from the rapid beta wave brain impulses to the slower, more meditative alpha wave state. As Ferguson explains:

> We are more attentive to the external world than the inner experience in the beta state. Meditation, reverie, relaxation, and other assorted psychotechnologies tend to increase the slower, *larger* brain waves known as the alpha and theta. . . . *In altered states of consciousness, fluctuations [in brain waves] may reach a critical level, large enough to provoke the shift into a higher level of organization.*[12] (emphasis hers)

She claims that in experiments involving shifts from beta waves to alpha waves, the "felt shift" as recorded in the EEG's is the point of what she calls "the new knowing."

Though New Agers like Ferguson use pseudoscientific jargon to explain these activities, Ruth Montgomery explains the exact same procedure from an openly occult position. And in fact the procedures are the same.

Invasion of the Body Snatchers?

Montgomery's book, *Strangers Among Us*, explains how beings from the spiritual side of life actually are taking possession of human beings and using them to help usher in the New Age of mankind. As improbable as this may sound, Montgomery calls these spirits Walk-Ins because they literally walk into the human's mind. The Bible refers to this as demonic. Her reports may or may not be true; however, many people believe what she has written. The connection between what New Age educators like Ferguson are saying and Montgomery's real-life version of the movie *Invasion of the Body Snatchers* is that both use intuition to tap into "the other world."

Montgomery interviewed a woman who was possessed by a Walk-In and asked how the spirit being was allowed to enter her. The woman responded that, "I began to pay more careful attention to my intuition."[13] Montgomery explains that by turning inward and reaching higher states of consciousness, a person opens himself to the entrance of the Walk-Ins.

I asked the Guides to explain the method used by spirits to reach those of us in physical body, and they replied: "We are attuned through something akin to thought waves, although of higher frequency, to some in the earth plane who are on similar frequency levels to our own; and as we wish to send to them, we fine-tune our own frequency to the earth cycle, and hence to that particular wavelength, so that we are in instant rapport with them, as they attune themselves to us through the so-called alpha state, we are able to trigger a response somewhat like a plane touching down to earth, landing, after soaring through the stratosphere. As we touch down, so to speak, we establish contact and meld with the minds of those with whom we are attuned.

In this way, we project pictures or symbols into their wavelength, and they reproject them as their own, unless they realize what is transpiring as you [Ruth Montgomery] do with the automatic writing. Were you not actively aware of this communication, we would be able to give you symbols or thought patterns, and as your personal radar reacted with them, you would assume that they were your own ideas and impressions, rather than having been passed along to you from this side.[14]

That is the occult explanation for what New Agers call enhancing intuition through altered states of consciousness.

Montgomery writes that once a person has opened himself up to the spirit guides, the individual will live with a sense of mission for ushering in the New Age. That person's life will seem normal on the exterior, but he will be absolutely devoted to carrying out his directed task. He will join forces with others who are also open to the higher consciousness and work together for the betterment of mankind.

This all sounds like the stuff of B-grade sci-fi movies, but educators steeped in New Age cosmology really believe it and actively work to infuse a watered-down version of this in public schools. More and more parents report that children are receiving lessons on enhancing creativity through developing greater intuition, a part of the spiritual globalist's agenda.

New Age globalists believe that introducing children to the "spirit beings" is essential to ushering in the new age of planetary consciousness. Rudhyar explains that, "In order to act in a precisely focused manner at the level of human existence, these super individual Beings require an agent."[15] New Agers believe that the "friends from the other side of life" are going to help bring about this utopia by actually working in and through a new generation of humans—the children of today.

These Walk-Ins will have a sense of mission concerning the building of this utopia. New Age writer Ferguson says the same thing as occult writer Montgomery. Ferguson calls this sense of mission a vocation—literally, a calling. She writes:

> Vocation is the process of making one's way toward something. It is a direction more than a goal. . . . The conspirators typically say they feel as if they are cooperating with events rather than controlling them. . . . By increasing our awareness of inner signals, the psychotechnologies promote a sense of vocation, an inner direction awaiting discovery and release.[16]

Hundreds of thousands of people are opening themselves up to a kind of soft-sell demon possession. Ferguson describes the infusion of occult cosmology as a conspiracy and states, "There is a conspiracy to make it less risky for people to experience transformation."[17] This idea was contained in a letter from Werner Erhard, Robert Fuller, and John Denver. Their letter stated:

> Acknowledging to ourselves and to you that we are all members of this 'conspiracy' to make the world a safer place for personal and social transformation brings us clarity of purpose and a sense of relatedness as we go about our business. In fact, the original meaning of conspiracy is to 'breathe together,' which expresses exactly what we have in mind.[18]

Believe it or not, John Denver is a major promoter of New Age thinking to school-age children. He has been through a variety of consciousness-altering sessions and believes he is helping usher in the coming New Age. At his New Age ranch, Windstar, courses in occult practices are held. Recently he hosted the visit of two Soviet officials at Windstar to talk about nuclear disarmament and future cooperation.[19]

Dealing with Occult Activity in Schools

By now you should have some idea of the disguises that occult mysticism uses in the classroom. The main thing to remember is not to be fooled by a "scientific" name. In fact, don't give much attention to the name at all. Look at the content and underlying assumptions. Also, ask yourself, "If introduced now, where will this program lead in five years?"

Education is in a constant quest for newness, and consequentially it is highly vulnerable to infusion of occult practices. Look beyond the program's stated goal. The stated purpose may be to build self-esteem, cope with stress, boost memory and creativity, or enhance affective development. So what? If occult means are used to achieve these goals, the means are unacceptable no matter how noble the end result. Occultism works. There is no doubt in my mind that engaging in such practices will help boost memory, deal with stress, and cure all kinds of personal problems. They offer a religious option to someone who is searching. I think you will have a hard time fighting such programs if you argue that they do not work. Rather, you should argue that they are religious because they deal with the nature of ultimate reality and how human values respond to that reality. You could also argue that attempts at getting in touch with "the spirits" is totally inappropriate for public education. Such occultism runs completely opposite of the religious values of a majority of Americans. To use schools as instruments for imposing such bizarre and dangerous religious thinking on unsuspecting children is absolutely unethical as well as illegal.

Finally, if your child is in a class that uses occult techniques, intercede for the child and teach the child how to pray for protection. In the world beyond what we can see is a vast battlefield of angelic warfare. By applying Biblical principles, Christians can be free from demonic oppression. However, it is important that discernment be applied to activities in the classroom. It is not recommended that parents yank children out of classes just because they are paranoid that "something" might happen. This book is intended to help you carefully examine programs that might dabble in New Age occultism. Do not depend on hearsay; check out the facts for yourself.

From a spiritual standpoint, the mystic vision of many global educators is the most dangerous aspect of their agenda. These spiritual globalists are using public schools as temples to propagate their occult dogma. Many school officials do not see the danger in New Age practices, which is all the more reason that the connection between global education and the occult be revealed at every level.

Christian parents need to also teach their children to arm themselves against the presence of demons on school campuses. The Bible clearly teaches that we are constantly in a sea of spiritual activity swirling all around us. This angelic conflict is intensified by teachers invoking the presence of spirit guides and mystical experiences. However, a child empowered by God's Holy Spirit can by prayer literally save an entire classroom of children from demonic oppression. The presence of these gentle, Christian warriors can do much in the battlefield of spiritual warfare. But parents must teach their children the art of spiritual hand-to-hand combat.

10

THE CALL FOR ONE WORLD GOVERNMENT

One of the principle lessons of our tragic century, which has seen so many millions of innocent lives sacrificed in schemes to improve the lot of humanity, is—beware intellectuals.[1]

Paul Johnson

Western Washington University offers a course called "Foundations of Education" that provides an example of how all the objectionable elements of global education are currently being taught. School districts around the nation seek education graduates from WWU. Not long ago the university made a commitment to indoctrinating its future teachers in global education. It makes sense for globalists to go after the young, impressionable college students and try to convince them of global utopianism. One of the major roadblocks to global education is the re-education of veteran teachers; obviously it is easier to mold the thinking of future ones.

Professor Philip Vander Velde teaches the course using two textbooks, *Global Mandate*, which he coedited, and *The Turning Point* by New Ager Fritjof Capra.

A brief examination of these two books reveals their endorsement of the objectionable ideas pointed out earlier. The future teachers enrolled in "Foundations of Education" face a continual barrage of curriculum which advocates changing our political structure to socialism and changing their personal religious beliefs to Eastern mysticism. If they do not do this, the authors claim, they imperil the future of mankind.

Global Mandate makes these assertions very clear. Regarding the need for a new religion to save the world, it states, "What is needed in a world faced with possible extinction is a new global spirituality."[2]

The kind of global spirituality being endorsed in *Global Mandate* is an odd blend of all religions with heavy leanings on Eastern mystic concepts. Exactly how religion will play a part in the new utopia is explained as follows: "Religions and quasi-religions will be able to exist in ecumenical relationship or in new synthesis, as in recent years individual spiritual explorers, such as the late Thomas Merton, have sought to combine Zen or Hinduism with Christianity."[3] It doesn't seem to bother these globalists that Hindus may object to infusing Christianity into their religion or that Christians will not allow their doctrine to be perverted. They simply assume that this is inevitable and thus acceptable.

Such blending of Hinduism and Christianity is typical of New Age thinking. However, the blend leans more toward Eastern mysticism than it does toward Christianity. The reason for the imbalance is that globalists like Fritjof Capra see Christianity as outdated and no longer useful for meeting today's needs. In his book, *The Turning Point*, future teachers are told the current resurgence of evangelical Christianity is simply "promoting medieval notions of reality." Certainly, future-minded, forward-thinking educators do not want to promote medieval notions of reality.

In the place of such dusty old religion, Capra offers educators a new faith that is "supported" by new discoveries in science.

> As Eastern thought has begun to interest a significant number of people, and meditation is no longer viewed with ridicule or suspicion, mysticism is being taken seriously even within the scientific community. An increasing number of scientists are aware that mystical thought provides a consistent and relevant philosophical background to the theories of contemporary science, a conception of the world in which the scientific discoveries of men and women can be in perfect harmony with their spiritual aims and religious beliefs.[4]

Consequently, anyone who does not hold to Eastern thought is now unscientific. These globalists consider Christians backward, unscientific, and a threat to world peace.

In Capra's mind, science cannot lead us to the Christian God; such a deity was adequate for the mechanistic world of centuries ago. Now, according to Capra, science will either lead us to the Buddha or to the Bomb, "and it is up to us to decide which path to take."[5] With such narrow alternatives as the *only* options, many children would think themselves foolish to not choose following the Buddha.

The *I Ching*

Capra believes that we must change our cultural values, including our political, ethical, emotional, and religious values. The basis for his new value system is derived from the ancient Chinese method of divination found in a book called the *I Ching*. Early in *The Turning Point*, he writes: "In our discussion of cultural values and attitudes throughout this book we will make extensive use of a framework that is developed in great detail in the *I Ching*, and that lies at the very basis of Chinese thought."[6]

I Ching divination is a method of foretelling the future by using a heap of yarrow sticks, some short and others long. The sticks are divided into heaps until a combination of short and long sticks forms patterns described in the *I Ching*. The *I Ching* contains sixty-four possible patterns and each formation has a different spiritual meaning for the future. Capra believes that this should form the basis of the future world society's religion.

These globalists preach a new "gospel" of salvation. They also preach that to reject "the very basis of Chinese thought" would be terribly ethnocentric. In other words, those who refuse to adopt Eastern mysticism are simply Western, ethnocentric bigots, and threats to the world society.

In another bizarre call for the redefinition of our religious foundations, Capra expounds the virtues of adopting the feminist spiritual view of goddess worship. After referring to the need for goddess worship, he states: "Thus the feminist movement will continue to assert itself as one of the strongest cultural currents of our time. Its ultimate aim is nothing less than a thorough redefinition of human nature."[7]

In *Global Mandate*, Vander Velde holds to the New Age/occult view that the earth is actually a living being, just as humans are living, and part of the cosmic, universal soul. These writers profess an intense ecological mindedness. However, when they talk of being ecologically minded, they are actually referring to a religious belief they call *deep ecology*, which involves getting in touch with the spirit of mother earth and ultimately making contact with the "cosmic mind." Capra states that participation in the deep ecological movement "will require a new philosophical and religious basis."[8]

The students' textbook emphatically states this highly religious viewpoint:

In the stratified order of nature, individual human minds are embedded in the larger minds of social and ecological systems, and these are integrated in the planetary mental system, which in turn must participate in some kind of universal or cosmic mind. This view of [the] mind has radical implications for our interactions with the natural environment, implications that are fully consistent with spiritual traditions.[9]

Such ideas certainly are not consistent with Christian spiritual traditions. But then these writers see orthodox Christianity as dead anyway. The students' second textbook, *The Turning Point*, states:

What we need, to prepare ourselves for the great transition we are about to enter, is a deep reexamination of the main premises and values of our culture, a rejection of those conceptual models that have outlived their usefulness, and a new recognition of some of the values discarded in previous periods of our cultural history.[10]

These global writers recognize that people will not give up their traditional religious beliefs easily; this will definitely cause problems for the utopian of the future. The prospective teachers read: "Men may cling to much of the language and symbolism of old creeds—secular and religious—but unless a new faith . . . overcomes the old ideologies and creates planetary synthesis, world government is doomed."[11]

Totalitarian Utopia

These writers insist that the future of the entire planet depends upon universal adoption of a new religion. On the surface, globalists talk of freeing humanity to achieve great things, but a careful reading of their works reveals a much different agenda. *Global Mandate* tells future teachers that the coming utopia will necessarily be somewhat totalitarian. The discussion of the need for a new religion reveals that:

> Groups of the world's population should, for a long time at least, be able to choose traditional ways. . . . What alone is necessary to create a humane world society is that all subcultures be . . . compatible with the world society's view of itself and of nature, and compatible with the unity of humanity and the earth. *To the extent that any cultural tendency denied this, it would be aberrant; to the extent that such a tendency was expressed in action, it would be subversive; and, to the extent that such a tendency might become powerful, it would be fought.* (emphasis added)[12]

Nothing will be tolerated that does not conform to "the world society's view of itself and of nature." This is a new way of asserting the Communist dogma, "The greatest good for the greatest number." The globalists' vision of the world society is socialistic; their view of nature is based on occult mysticism. Nonconformists are considered aberrant or deviant, their practices subversive, and threats to the world society. And if the will of the people empowers a nonconformist, he will be fought.

Ironically, these writers accuse their opponents of desires for such totalitarianism. In a vicious attack on conservatives in America, one writer for Global Mandate rhetorically asks:

> Whether it can be just coincidental that those who are urging women to go back to so-called traditional male-dominated roles in the home under strong-man rule—as the New Right so urges—are at the same time working for political strong-man rule, for a small male elite with little or no respect for the civil and economic rights of the mass of not only women but also men.[13]

Ignorant attacks on conservatives should be recognized as attacks on those holding particular religious views in

America as well. Global writers single out for attack fundamental Christians who have inherited the label "New Right." This should be expected. Conservative Christians will not fit into globalists' utopia politically or religiously. These conservative Christians will not accept socialism over capitalism, nor will they voluntarily accept a synthesis of their faith with Eastern mysticism—even if they were convinced it would save the world. Foundational to Christian doctrine are Jesus' words: "What shall it profit a man, if he shall gain the whole world, and lose his own soul?" (Mark 8:36).

New World Order

The new teachers coming out of Western Washington University will be teaching citizenship education. Most people assume this means teaching students how to be good citizens of our country. Concepts of patriotism, loyalty, pride, and responsibility toward those of our nation come to mind. However, globalists who train future educators have different ideas about citizenship education. As the *Global Mandate* states: "Citizenship education, found in every respectable nation claiming to be civilized, is replete with curricula through which it teaches its citizens chauvinism, patriotism, and nationalism: the by-products of a world view which pits man against his fellow human beings."[14]

Citizenship eduction of the global nature means teaching the shortcomings of our nation and the wonderful vision of the future world society. "Nation-states have outlived their usefulness, and a new world order is necessary if we are to live in harmony with each other. . . . The task of re-ordering our traditional values and institutions should be one of the major educational objectives of our schools."[15]

Like John Goodlad, Vander Velde shows little regard for the public trust. Parents send their children to school with the assumption that parental values are being upheld or at least are not being eroded. Vander Velde turns his back on such trust and wants educators to "re-order our traditional values." Since he sees this re-ordering as the major objective of education, it is logical to assume that he teaches prospective public school teachers to make this their primary objective. Education to them is not merely helping a person develop his faculties to such a degree that he becomes a fulfilled and significant participant in society. They want to be the engineers of utopia, and they pursue their goals with a religious passion. They believe that if their mission is hindered, it means automatic global suicide.

Transition to the World State

The students' textbook also instructs a gradual re-ordering of traditional values. But eventually, "a new political order of control over human relationships will come into being. This clearly implies that a national sovereignty, which is the basis of the current nation-state system . . . can be whittled away."[16]

When this gradual departure from the nation-state system has been achieved, these globalists comment that, "Eventually, of course, the United Nations or some successor organization will have to evolve into a true world government."[17] These authors reveal that a ten-year transition plan has been developed in a book called *World Peace Through World Law*. It suggests "a teaching model that could contribute to the needed transformation."[18]

In *Global Mandate*, William Boyer writes enthusiastically about the many educational avenues that globalists are infiltrating within the system. World-order workshops are commonplace at curriculum conferences and social studies meetings. The National Council for the Social Studies has recognized that peace education and world order education are legitimate programs. For those public school educators who still believe that global education amounts to nothing more than studies in international trade and economics, *Global Mandate* sets the record straight:

> Under the name of global education there are some who have introduced the idea that our schools need to teach the history and culture of other peoples and nations so that we can sell them more American-made goods. This is anything but global education; it is, in fact, crass material-ism and mercantile imperialism perpetuated under the cloak of global education. Global education should be more than our interest in selling more goods, or our con-cern about establishing better trade relations. . . . It should be humanistic in its strategies to be used in the classroom discourse. Above all, . . . [it] should be critical of our his-tory of aggression and violence, of the social institutions supporting the values and beliefs contributing to vio-lence. . . . [It] needs to bring into the process of schooling a well balanced interplay of theory and practice on how we can contribute to the creation of a new world order.[19]

Based upon their own writings, these globalists are guilty of subversion and treason. They aggressively fly in the face of public trust and push forward to indoctrinate teachers and children in their elitist, utopian dogma. They do not want to teach children *how* to think; they want to indoctrinate young minds in *what* to think.

What to Think: World Socialism

Globalists claim that the key political concept of the world must be socialism. Giving no other alternative, Professor Vander Velde states that, "we can no longer afford eco-nomic competition."[20] That statement sets the tone for all political discussion in *Global Mandate*. Further in the text-book, in a discussion of political and economic systems, he states that: "A system found to be sufficiently obsolete and pathological requires fundamental redesign rather than a face-lifting; that system must be either eliminated or fundamentally transformed through substitution."[21]

Globalist teachers at Western Washington University want to see capitalism eliminated and socialism instituted. To them, this is not an option but an absolute imperative. They assert that: "Equalizing economic levels is necessary. . . . Controlling economic growth and redistributing assets on a world scale obviously involves . . . control, and development on a world scale . . . as well as a system of de facto international taxation."[22]

Remember, these writers are not economic theorists; they are teacher trainers. They are using the public school system to circumvent the democratic process. The American people are not being given the opportunity to vote on whether or not a socialistic government should be instituted. These educators hope that by indoctrinating future generations with socialistic dogma, adults who have gone through twelve years of this political education eventually will vote to approve the system designed by their educational "fathers."

Most global writers use less threatening—and less obvious—terms for socialism such as *economic justice* or *equitable distribution of human values*, but an author in *Global Mandate* states with glowing pride that, "Socialism from the start has opposed nationalism and summoned 'proletarians of all countries unite.'"[23] In explaining the methods of instituting socialism in different cultures, the author acknowledges that, "differing 'shades' of socialism will be preferred."[24]

Global Cultural Revolution

Capra's book hits the future educators in this course with the salvation of socialism. He calls for political and economic upheaval that will mirror Mao Tse-tung's cultural revolution on a global scale. In describing what action this new world government will have to take, he states that: "This will include, among many other measures, the decentralization of populations and industrial activities, the dismantling of large corporations and other social institutions, the redistribution of wealth, and the creation of flexible, resource-conserving technologies."[25]

His call for decentralizing populations appears to be a call for forced evacuation of urban dwellers to rural areas. Of course, these social manipulators always have the good of the masses in mind. History is replete with examples of such leaders: Lenin, Stalin, Pol Pot, Mao Tse-tung, and Hitler. It just so happened that a few million people had to be removed to insure the health of the whole society. These new totalitarians have already assured us that those who oppose the good of the world society will be considered aberrant, subversive, and will be fought.

Academic Freedom v. Intellectual Honesty

Global educators are guilty of the worst kind of academic abuse. They hide behind academic freedom while they use their position to bypass the democratic system. They sacrifice intellectual honesty and substitute political indoctrination.

Academic freedom carries with it the necessity for intellectual honesty. These educators care little for such responsibility. Claiming the "higher" calling of saving humanity from the disastrous scenario they themselves have painted, they knowingly abuse their position and seek to politically indoctrinate society through its most defenseless members—children.

They skew their perspective of the world to support an insupportable position. Their opinions are taught as imperatives. There are no options. There is no discussion. Total acceptance or total destruction are the alternatives offered to schoolchildren.

An Appeal to Reasonable People

Reasonable educators and parents must awaken to what is happening. The majority of educators certainly do not realize the motives and goals of global education. Most educators are simply trying to do the best job they can in meeting the needs of children and society. They recognize the problems facing the world and truly want to make some kind of significant impact in their world. This is commendable. But these same educators must begin to ask global educators tough questions based on thorough research. Passive acceptance of global dogma is dangerous. Of course, total capitulation to global educators' strange vision of the future would cripple the individual and society. These globalists are utopian dreamers totally out of touch with reality. Even if such a world state were to be installed, it would not build the grand Garden of Eden they so desire. The real danger in implementing global education is that a generation of children will be wasted on this scheme for social engineering. These *experimental* children will be cut-off from their cultural roots in Western civilization; they will be set adrift in a sea of ambiguity. Christian children who hold to certain absolute convictions will be victimized by these programs. This experimental generation will not be educated to use their faculties to truly make their own decisions; instead, they will be encouraged to accept socialistic dogma and Eastern mystic religions, at first in watered-down forms. Decision-making skills will, of course, be encouraged, as long as such skills fit into a particularly narrow mind-set.

Is this why parents send their children to school? Is this why taxpayers support public schools? Is there any doubt that the platform of global education would be completely rejected on the voting ballot? By trying to dishonestly sneak their agenda into public schools, global educators are endangering the entire public school system. Our public schools are too valuable to risk such public rejection. If public educators do not reject global education, the public will reject the system.

Beware of the classroom masquerade.

How You Can Help

The situation is far from hopeless. Through neglect we have allowed our public schools to be overrun by a small minority of elitist, social engineers. The problem can be corrected.

At the university level, the remedy is to cut funding for programs sponsoring global education. Those who support universities through large endowment funds should be presented with well-documented reports on global education think-tanks in the universities they support. Local legislators responsible for state funding of higher education could also apply pressure on universities to stop global education.

At the secondary and elementary level, funding must also be cut for global education by means of the local school board. Obtain the sources mentioned in this book and document your own research. Remember that educating students to understand the world is not the issue. The issue is the inappropriateness of current global education course material. Teachers and administrators must take the responsibility of informing their colleagues and school boards of the dangers.

Educators, parents, and school boards need to work together to develop policies that specifically exclude unpatriotic, subversive, or occult programs.

Parents need to be three things: informed, organized, and active. First, be informed. Know the facts. This book is designed to be a starting point. You should be able to track down the sources I have used. I have offered arguments that can be used against global education.

Secondly, get organized. One parent crying in the wilderness will not usually have the necessary volume. An organized group of parents is needed. You can recruit help from contacts in your church, synagogue, PTA, civic club, or other community centers. Business leaders would be concerned because of global educations' anticapitalistic stance.

Starting a Public School Awareness committee in your church is a good way of getting organized. A Public School Awareness (PSA) church committee is a systematic way for a church to stay abreast of what is happening in its local public schools. The PSA committee can be effective with as few as one or two people in it. Of course, it is desirable to have more people involved, but you may need to start with just yourself.

Public School Awareness committees have been started in churches throughout the country. The PSA committee idea was developed by Citzens for Excellence in Education—a national ministry with years of experience in helping thousands of concerned citizens like yourself. A PSA committee kit can be obtained for your church. The kit contains six audio cassettes, a workbook/manual to show you exactly how to get involved with the schools, Parent Action Guides, bulletin inserts on education, and a whole host of helpful materials. It is a uniquely practical way to begin impacting your local public schools.

With a PSA committee in place, you can keep the rest of your church informed as to what is being taught in public schools. The PSA kit outlines a five step process for successfully finding out what children are learning and how you can get involved if you don't like what you see.

Christians have recognized for many years the importance of improving public school education. Since 90 percent of the church sends its children to public schools, it is imperative that Christians get involved with what and how those church children are being taught. Until the introduction of the PSA kit, Christian involvement in pubic schools has been disorganized and for the most part ineffective. Now with the clear guidance of the PSA committee kit, you can impact the schools with the positive help that the Christian community can offer. (See the last page of the book for how to receive more information on the PSA committee kit.)

Finally, get active. Meet on a regular basis for research, strategy formulation, and support. Contact your school board members in a nonthreatening setting outside the school board meeting. Most board members will not effectively interact with parents regarding concerns while in the formal school board setting. Two parents should meet over coffee with one school board member. Women tend to have greater success with school board members who are women; males work better with the male school board members. Although this might seem sexist, it is also a reality.

You may be met with arguments that your district's global education does not contain any of "that bad stuff." Do not reduce your research efforts without fully examining all the material used. You will need to go so far as to follow up on the origin of the material. Then research the philosophy of that institution; read other publications the author has produced.

All of this admittedly takes work, but who else will do it? The future of your children and the future of American society as we know it rests on what you do locally. You must act on your vision of a public school system free from global educators' manipulation and prevent the revision of the values our founding fathers saw as the key to our nation's greatness.

BLOWING THE WHISTLE ON GLOBAL EDUCATION

W hat follows is an internal document from the U.S. Department of Education. It has never before been published in its entirety and serves as a summary of much of what has been detailed throughout the book.

Greg Cunningham's report for the U.S.D.E. focuses mainly on the Center for Teaching International Relations' "World Citizen Curriculum." It serves to illustrate the danger of implementing global education programs that lack objective balance. Written during the Reagan administration, some of the people mentioned have, of course, changed posts. The problem of imbalanced global education remains however.

The 120 footnotes in the report have been edited for ease of reading. If you would like a complete documentation of this appendix, write to: Citizens for Excellence in Education, Box 3200, Costa Mesa, CA 92628.

What Is Global Education?

An important phenomenon is sweeping America's schools, and its significance cannot be overstated. Although it's known by a variety of names, the concept is most commonly referred to as *global education*, and the rate at which it is being "infused" into K-12 curricula is rapidly accelerating.

While the term means substantially different things to different people, there are several elements common to most *global* curriculum guides. The first of these involves the teaching procedure. Globalism is not a course, but rather a new way of teaching existing courses. That "new way" is designed to present all course material from an international point of view. In its most useful form, this new perspective would enhance student appreciation of cultural diversity and philosophical pluralism, encourage transnational cooperation, teach conflict management skills, foster commitment to the responsible consumption of natural resources, develop strategies for controlling environmental pollution, sensitize students to the interdependency of the world's people and systems, and emphasize the importance of human rights for everyone.

Global education curriculum materials are being published and promoted by scores of organizations across the country, and the concept has attracted the staunch support of prominent educational institutions, such as the National Association of Elementary School Principals, the American Association of School Administrators, the American Federation of Teachers (labor union), the Council of Chief State School Officers, the National Association of State Boards of Education, the National Education Association (labor union), the Parent-Teachers Association (PTA), and the National School Boards Association.

Typical of many of the groups generating and encouraging the use of these materials is the Center for Teaching International Relations (CTIR) at the University of Denver. It conducts teacher workshops, teaches academic courses, produces publications, provides consulting services to public schools, offers graduate degree programs and holds summer institutes. It derives support chiefly from the above activities, the University of Denver, and the Danforth Foundation. It was founded in 1968.

Using basic networking principles, CTIR has cooperated with kindred spirits among public school faculties, and in so doing has worked its programs into the course offerings of many Western school districts. Over the last decade, its programs have been completed by some five hundred teachers per year. Many of these participants are employed by school districts in states far beyond the Rocky Mountain West.

In a world that is shrinking at an exponential rate, one might ask what reasonable person would oppose efforts to teach children about the world beyond our borders. The issue is, unfortunately, not that simple.

Social scientists often define politics as the process by which societies decide who gets what, when, where, how, and in what amounts. By that definition, every issue raised by any program of global education is a political issue—and often a political issue of the most controversial sort.

Education Versus Indoctrination

This paper focuses heavily on CTIR because it is one of the largest publishers of global education materials in the United States. I examined a dozen or more CTIR curriculum guides in their entirety. The objective was to review the more controversial subject areas for intellectual honesty, objective inquiry, and awareness of and tolerance for countervailing points of view. The outcome was sadly disappointing on each criterion.

No social science text can be all things to all readers, and in all fairness to CTIR, many parents would find much of the University of Denver material to be relatively innocuous. Many of these curriculum guides, however, deal with emotionally charged political and spiritual issues. Why? Because the authors are prone to selectively exclude inconvenient historical facts. Information which is inconsistent with the desired point of view simply disappears. Philosophical perspectives that are anathema to liberal political thought are either caricatured or omitted. Students might easily conclude that controversial theories are actually established facts. They could conclude that complex problems have only one legitimate solution.

These deficiencies might be remedied with the addition of factual information and some diversity of philosophical thought (or by candidly renouncing the fraudulent representation that these readings constitute a "balanced" offering).

Of greater concern, however, is the material which seeks to elicit private familial information by probing children psychologically. Many parents believe that such activities are challenging parental authority and usurping their prerogatives. In a related area, CTIR's *death education* activities are so insensitive to the problem of teenage suicide that whole sections should be deleted.

Similar criticisms can be found in an essay entitled "Globaloney" (*American Spectator*, May 1986), authored by U.S. Department of Education Under Secretary Gary Bauer and Assistant Secretary Chester E. Finn. The authors explain that their interest in global education "was triggered by the maudlin one-worldism that has seized the social studies establishment." They conclude that teaching texts of this sort are marred by defects which include "relativism, bad history joined to ideology, events without causes or consequences," and books which "falter badly" when dealing with "modern times."

A "New World Order"

Some globalists have, at least in a general sense, been quite candid in conceding the value-laden nature of their objectives. CTIR, for instance, boldly proclaims its quest for a "new world order" and dismisses those who resist the creation of this New Age millennium as "miseducators." Another proponent of global education, writing in the November/December issue of *Curriculum Review*, states up front that "globalists want to change attitudes." The Northwest Regional Educational Laboratory equates "serious global educators" with "change agents . . . that influence development of attitudes." The writers go on to discuss the "political socialization of young people" and suggest that "visibility lends credibility to a position regardless of what it is." They conclude with the contention that global education is a "worldview" and declare that "the future is not to be predicted but made." In this same connection, one of their recommended readings is *The Development of Political Attitudes in Children* by Hess and Torney.

Once children have been "socialized" with sufficient intensity to inculcate the "political attitudes" which are necessary for the creation of a "new world order," what are they to do with this novel outlook? CTIR emphasizes that it is most satisfying to be "an active doer" rather than someone to whom things are being done. In another text they call for students' "commitment to action" while challenging them to "dare to think the unthinkable" and "go for the works." Their section on nuclear conflict directs teachers to explain that "sharing opinions is a social responsibility in a democracy. Only by letting others know how we feel can we hope to change opinions." But CTIR wants students to do more than merely share opinions. They suggest the circulation of political petitions, the drafting and publication of press releases, and the staging of press conferences. Students are further encouraged to join liberal political organizations and form similar groups of their own.

Merely establishing the fact that many global educators want to turn schoolchildren into political activists to achieve a new world order is less significant, however, than is the *substance* of that "brave new world" and the *techniques* being advocated to indoctrinate the children who are to be its founders.

"Peace" Without Freedom?

CTIR's most doctrinaire texts deal with global conflict and nuclear war. These topics are intensely controversial because most Americans have traditionally valued their freedom more highly than their lives (hence a democracy now entering its third century). Many proponents of "deterrence through strength" believe that it is hypocritical for pacifists to enjoy the freedom that has been secured by the mortal sacrifice of previous generations while refusing to risk that same sacrifice for generations yet unborn. Some would even argue that such Americans don't deserve to be free. Many advocates of the nuclear freeze, however, believe that the loss of freedom as we know it is preferable to loss of life on the scale they envision pursuant to global war. So a *hawk* is incensed that the *doves* are risking his freedom to save their lives, while a *dove* is appalled that the *hawks* are jeopardizing his existence to preserve their liberty. Each, in essence, believes that the other seeks to imperil that which he holds most dear.

It would be inaccurate to suggest that CTIR materials are totally devoid of information opposing the nuclear freeze; however, most objective readers would find a distinct pro-freeze bias in the curriculum guides.

Conspicuous by its absence, for instance, is any discussion of the value of freedom as a concept worthy of ultimate sacrifice. Life after global war is invariably described in the most horrific possible terms, but the quality of life after the loss of liberty is never even mentioned. In one introductory section, a child is quoted as saying, "It has been shown me how stupid some adults can be. If they know it could easily kill them [nuclear advances and the arms race], I have no idea why they support it." Nothing appearing in any CTIR materials is likely to remedy that child's ignorance. Civil defense is derided as a naive fantasy in a poorly balanced article; the article fails to examine the Soviet conviction that such preparedness is crucial to the achievement of foreign policy objectives. Why would the Soviets invest so heavily in the creation of such elaborate safeguards? CTIR material never seriously considers the question.

In a simulation based on the Cuban missile crisis, the text instructs students that their goal is to "resolve this conflict." The material lacks even an intimation that the *outcome* of the conflict might be more important than merely resolving it at *any price.*

CTIR's treatment of other defense-related issues is also pacifistic, and in some cases, to the point of being capitulatory. A listing of nine strategies for resolving conflict includes eight which involve at least some degree of surrender (role reversal, nonviolence, pacifism, bargaining, compromise, consensus, ignoring, and accommodating). The application of force is referred to only disparagingly with a parenthetical note asserting that force "usually doesn't resolve a conflict, but instead changes or delays the conflict." It may be fair to assert that force should generally be viewed as the alternative of last resort, but to dismiss this option out-of-hand seems a crude attempt to proselytize children.

Great emphasis is given to the playing of a so-called world game designed by globalist Buckminster Fuller in which "any resort to armed conflict immediately disqualifies players." The game is played with a curious graphic called the "Dymaxion World Map" which invariably depicts the United States upside-down.

Ideological Differences

Global educators generally regard conflict to be a product of ideological differences, ideological misunderstandings, the maldistribution of resources, international competition, and nationalism. Along with nationalism, they include ethnocentrism and national elitism. While there is nothing particularly unusual in these points of view, the solutions offered to ameliorate the conflict supposedly spawned by each of these are another matter.

With regard to ideological differences, globalists often suggest the imagined importance of teaching students to become comfortable with ambiguity. No mention is made, however, of the skill and consistency with which totalitarian adversaries employ ambiguity as a weapon to paralyze democracies. Painful experience has taught the West that public opinion reaches consensus only in the face of threats which are clearly defined.

Defense Secretary Casper W. Weinberger recently observed that:

> We cannot assume that the enemy . . . will necessarily do us the favor of furnishing warning that is unambiguous. . . . Indeed Soviet military doctrine puts great emphasis on deception and surprise. . . . Our forces and those of our allies must be prepared to respond to warning indicators that are highly ambiguous. . . . Being prepared to respond only to warning that is unambiguous means being prepared for the kind of warning we are least likely to get.

Are the world's problems black and white? Of course not, and students must be taught to analyze the shades of gray that package most dilemmas. But tolerance is hardly a satisfactory substitute for analysis.

Consider the extent to which ambiguity incapacitated administration efforts to persuade Congress that Nicaragua's Sandinista regime was undermining stability in Central America. Should funding for the Contras be approved? On the strength of what evidence of Sandinista wrongdoing? The president established that the Soviets were taking U.S. arms captured by the North Vietnamese from the South Vietnamese and routing them through the Nicaraguans to the Salvadoran Communist rebels, who were attempting to bring down the Duarte government. Here was Soviet-crafted ambiguity at its crippling best. But then Nicaraguan president Daniel Ortega misstepped by allowing himself to be photographed in the comradely embrace of Mikhail Gorbachev while soliciting aid from Soviet bloc nations. The ambiguity was suddenly clarified for many Americans. As public opinion coalesced into majority sentiment, the funding was approved. An attack on U.S. interests at Pearl Harbor is easy to understand. An attack on those same interests in Southeast Asia or Central America is much less easily fathomed.

Teaching healthy *skepticism* concerning ambiguity might be more useful than encouraging tolerance for the murky tactics which the Libyans, for example, have so effectively employed to immobilize or limit the West's response to state-sponsored terrorism.

A related remedy suggested by globalists to mitigate conflict arising from ideological difference is to avoid being judgmental. In a September 22, 1985, *New York Times* article, Julia To-Dutka said of globalism: "The future of the world depends on our willingness to suspend our own judgment of thoughts that we do not as yet understand, feelings with which we are not yet able to identify, and actions that we do not as yet approve."

The need for open-mindedness concerning diverse perspectives cannot reasonably be disputed, but few global educators stop there. Some assert the absence of absolutes of any sort. What they seem to be saying is that they simply don't like the conventional values which are commonly recognized as moral absolutes. However, they refuse to openly repudiate traditional morality to avoid the appearance of radicalism. They further cloud this denial of the existence of moral absolutes by positing "maxims" of their own formulation (obviously based on absolute assumptions) in almost every realm of human endeavor (i.e., avoidance of conflict as ultimate good). The CTIR curriculum guide entitled *Teaching About U.S. History*, for instance, exhorts students to examine "images and values based on new evidence" and act "on values in light of a new consciousness that has arisen about the United States as a result of examining its past comparatively." Values which are an intrinsic part of our heritage are referred to as *old* values—obviously connoting obsolescence—while the mores of the Third World are described as *traditional* values—suggesting that which is worthy of veneration and preservation.

In keeping with the contradictory denial of the existence of moral absolutes is the frequent and approving reference to the controversial process of *values clarification*. The authors of a recently published book entitled *Classrooms in Crisis* define the concept in terms of the following assumptions:

1. There are no universal or absolute truths (i.e., truths that are true for anybody, anywhere, at anytime).

2. There are no universal or absolute values.

3. There are no knowable objective criteria for distinguishing right from wrong, good from evil, humane from inhumane, just from unjust, moral from immoral.

4. All value judgments are purely subjective.

5. Any opinion about right and wrong is as good as any other opinion.

6. There are no intrinsic values (i.e., no values that are in essence better or worse than other values).

7. People can have moral *beliefs* (we all do), but no one can have any moral *knowledge* (i.e., a certainly reliable way to distinguish true from false, or right from wrong moral beliefs).

This moral relativism is evident in the Teacher Resource Guide of the CTIR *World Citizen Curriculum*: "Do we sometimes have a tendency to define our values and behaviors as 'right' or 'correct' and determine the others' values and behaviors as 'wrong' or 'weird?' Is any one person or culture 'right' or 'wrong'?" The preferred answer is obvious.

Former U.N. Ambassador Jean Kirkpatrick coined another name for *moral relativism* when applied to international relations. She calls it *moral equivalence*. Simply stated, the term stands for the proposition that the ethical principles on which any sovereignty structures its social, economic, and political systems—as well as the policy objectives which flow from those structures—are morally indistinguishable from those of any other sovereignty.

French author Jean Francosia Revel comments on a variant of this concept in his book, *How Democracies Perish*. He observes that a large body of public opinion in the Netherlands recently held that the Dutch government lacked a moral right to criticize Communist repression or Soviet imperialism in such countries as Poland or Afghanistan: "as long as housing conditions in Amsterdam failed to meet the highest standards of modern comfort, as long as women remained exploited and the legal rights of heterosexual married couples are denied to homosexual married couples."

Global educators also treat the Soviets with deference. They may not be apologists for Soviet atrocities in explicit terms, but globalists spare no effort in their attempts to place the best possible face on the motives and behavior of the Soviet state.

CTIR also implicitly analogizes the Soviet Union and the United States with street gangs, essentially indistinguishable from one another. They explicitly do the same concerning the KGB and CIA with no attempt to separate their methods or purposes.

Even more strangely, a related passage describes members of the Warsaw Pact and other unnamed nations as "friends" of the U.S.S.R. in the same sense that members of NATO are friends of the United States. CTIR might more honestly have compared Soviet reaction to the embryonic emergence of freedom in Czechoslovakia in 1968 with the U.S. response to France's decision to withdraw from NATO in the early sixties. Or what about the "friendly" Soviet practice of ravaging the economies of Eastern European countries (reported in the April 28, 1986 issue of *Time*, "Communism's Old Men," p. 41) by pirating away their best scientists and engineers to work on Soviet projects while selling Soviet oil to these satellite nations at three times the world price? But which nations *could* fairly be described as "friends" of the U.S.S.R.? Poland? Hungary? Can a relationship maintained at gunpoint be accurately characterized as "friendship"? Global revisionists are confusing the world they desire with the world whose realities they choose to deny. In so doing, they are inadvertently, or by design, parroting the Soviet propaganda line and misleading students in the process.

[Former] U.S. Education Secretary William Bennett criticized "moral equivalence" in a recent speech to the Shavano Institute of Hilsdale College in Michigan.

> Surely one explanation for the fact that democratic values no longer seem to command the assent they once did is that for many years now the teaching of social studies in

our schools has been dominated by cultural relativism. The notion that the attempt to draw meaningful distinctions between opposing traditions is a judgment which all virtuous and right-minded people must sternly condemn.

One social studies series for elementary schools, for example, advises the teacher that the material aims to "decrease inclination toward egocentrism, ethnocentrism and stereotyping." But what *this means, it turns out, is more than teaching children that all cultures and traditions are not the same. It means teaching that all cultures and traditions are equally valid, that there are not real criteria for good and bad, right and wrong, noble and base* (emphasis added).

Ideological Misunderstanding

Globalists also see ideological misunderstanding as a source of conflict. One might imagine that the "critical thinking" skills global educators often claim to be teaching would help ameliorate misunderstanding, but after reviewing their curriculum guides, it can be seen that "critical thinking" does not mean systematic analysis. Many globalists seem committed to emotionalizing public policy decision-making in a way that renders rational evaluation impossible. One remarkable essay in the CTIR *Nuclear Conflict* text, for instance, proposes that to fully impress the president with the magnitude of his intended action, he should not be permitted to resort to nuclear defense until he has killed one of his own aides with a butcher knife. This, to remove the firing codes contained in a capsule that has been implanted in the aide's chest cavity. Is this an attempt to encourage students to think clearly or feel passionately about the complex issue of nuclear deterrence?

Later in the same text, it is suggested that students "don't need to understand the global political situation or the details of the arms race." They should just "give up blaming" and "find a Russian and get to know her or him." There are many educators who would argue that much Soviet behavior is blameworthy and that students should know it. They would further dispute the contentions that students "don't need to understand the global political situation or the details of the arms race" and would add that the level of one's understanding of such things is inversely proportional to one's inclination toward "globalism." They might conclude by observing that "getting to know a Russian," desirable though that may be for a variety of cultural reasons, is totally irrelevant to questions of public policy. The average Russian is isolated from the real world by a government he lacks the *voice* to influence, the *knowledge* to analyze, or the *will* to reform.

Another section of the same curriculum guide describes the destructive impact of the atomic weapons "dropped on Japan" but withholds equally relevant information regarding the Japanese. Japanese military resistance became fanatical to the point of suicidal frenzy as Allied forces neared the Japanese home islands. Experts predicted additional loss of life in excess of one million people if the war was ended with an amphibious invasion by Allied ground troops. The "bomb" not only prevented this carnage but also quite possibly prevented the disappearance of much or all of Japan behind the Iron Curtain. Had participation in a Japanese land-war enabled the Soviets to force an Eastern European-style partition of these islands, the results could easily have been more devastating to the Japanese than a dozen atomic bombs.

Focusing only on the destructive impact of these two bombs is an unbalanced and misleading presentation. The question of the legitimacy of the use of any weapon can only fairly be resolved by examining the consequences of its use and disuse. Do we want to recruit "anti-nuke" zealots, or do we want to teach national security policy-making?

Children need to understand these realities but are unlikely to do so if globalist curricula are their only source of information.

Operant Conditioning

Instead of teaching rigorous historical analysis, CTIR's *Teaching About U.S. History* notes that "the vast number of students today are visually oriented" and urges teachers to "take advantage of the fact [by cutting out pictures that relate to history] rather than fight it." Don't fight reluctance to read? Pictures can obviously offer emotional impact, but standing alone, they can also be misleading and reinforce lethargy. They can never compensate for the absence of well-balanced essays. Is CTIR's objective operant conditioning or critical thinking?

Consistent with its heavy emphasis on emotionalism, CTIR's *World Citizen Curriculum, Teacher Resource Guide* instructs teachers to organize "an experimental exercise in which students participate in leading and being led on a blindfolded walk." The activity focuses "on the need for trust between people and cultures" without even mentioning the value of circumspection in evaluating international motives and behavior. Some parents would no doubt question this aggrandizement of "blind trust" as an approach to foreign relations with, say, the State of Iran.

A more useful exercise for promoting student understanding might have been for CTIR to explain the Soviet definition of the word *peace* as it appears in the *Nuclear Conflict* material. How does it differ from the U.S. meaning? According to former Soviet Ambassador Arkady Shevchenko, now defected to the West, Communists define the term as the absence of class struggle which abates when society embraces the Marxist-Leninist dialectic. In essence, *peace* is possible only when resistance to communism ends. How many

Americans would choose "world peace" in those terms? How many students know the difference?

Welfare—Foreign or Domestic

"Maldistribution" of world resources also receives simplistic treatment as a cause of world conflict. A reader could easily conclude that U.S. selfishness is largely responsible for this "maldistribution," as students are asked what they would personally be willing to give up to rectify Third World destitution. It is vaguely suggested that our life style at home contributes to deprivation abroad. It is also hinted that world poverty is compounded by "inadequate" U.S. foreign aid. Our contribution, as a percentage of gross national product, is compared unfavorably with aid levels from other industrialized nations. The redistribution focus which pervades this section is illustrated by the encouragement it gives students to "discuss some ways one might institute . .

policies to implement the distribution of food, clothing and shelter throughout the world on a 'more equal' basis." Students are asked to define "human needs" in terms designed to discourage the inclusion of military aid. In a "foreign aid game" designed by CTIR, defense assistance available for developing nations is limited to the "neutron bomb, MX missile, nuclear weapons, a squadron of F-14 fighter jets and Trident missiles." The fact that these items are unsuitable for use by Third World countries and so expensive that any one of them would consume many times the foreign aid appropriation of these nations, ensures that students will not request military aid for their "countries." Defense related items that are less expensive and more crucial to the maintenance of a nation's sovereignty are categorically excluded from the "game." (But then globalists barely value sovereignty.)

Nowhere is the redistributionist mentality more apparent than in the testimony of a welfare recipient decrying the "inadequacy" of available benefits. Welfare systems must obviously concern themselves with the effective delivery of aid to those least able to provide for themselves, but a dual responsibility of those same systems is the avoidance of fraud that robs both the poor and the taxpayers. Do globalists discuss the problem of welfare cheating at either the international or domestic level? No.

An equally unbalanced manifestation of this leveling impulse is found in the *World Citizen Curriculum's* tacit suggestion that the U.S. should provide "guaranteed employment" and "guaranteed health care."

CTIR could replace bias with balance by assigning, for instance, readings from Charles Murray's highly acclaimed book *Losing Ground* (Basic Books, Inc., 1984). This volume thoughtfully examines American social policy between 1950 and 1980 with the provocative conclusion that well-meaning but wrong-headed programs have brutalized short-term beneficiaries by making long-term victims. We have in essence "killed" our welfare recipients with irresponsible kindness. Says Murray: "The real contest about the direction of social policy is not between people who want to cut budgets and people who want to help. When reforms finally do occur, they will happen not because stingy people have won, but because generous people have stopped kidding themselves."

Jingoism?

Another broad category of conflict sources includes elitism, egocentricism, and ethnocentrism which, to a globalist, add up to nationalism. But what of the traditional notion that America has a proper leadership role to play in the world?

No effort is spared in the attempt to disabuse students of that "primitive" misapprehension.

Although they lean in that direction, most globalists stop just short of condemning patriotism. The Northwest Regional Educational Laboratory, however, asserts that a "highly nationalistic" person is unqualified to function as a global educator.

Which World?

What emerges from many globalist materials is an indisputable "one-world" objective. Using a subliminal but effective technique seen frequently in CTIR materials, the *World Citizen Curriculum* lists a series of seven innocuous progressions, each comprised of three evolutionary levels, with the seventh predicting the ultimate transcendence of international organizations over nations. The same document asks students to complete a "what if" exercise whose scenarios are worded and arranged in a configuration suggestive of the preferred response. One policy proposal is the removal of national borders, and the other is the power of a world court to impose and enforce the collection of fines. Further on, disapproval is expressed for "national sovereignty (refusal to give up power to global organizations)."

The desirability of cooperation vis-à-vis competition is a recurrent theme in globalist literature. As is so often the case in materials of this type, the problem lies not with the substance of the abstract statement. The real concern centers on the lack of balance. Cooperation is generally to be preferred to competition, but the latter can be a constructive force where cooperation is impossible or would not be helpful. CTIR texts seek to convey the halcyon impression that gaps between hopelessly irreconcilable opposites (socialism and capitalism, for instance) can always be closed with the application of vague one-world principles to which little more than oblique reference is ever made. Once again, the world is painted in the fanciful colors of the wishful thinker, who is ever oblivious to hard reality.

Hostility Toward Capitalism

Some CTIR lesson plans view free enterprise economics with disapproval (ranging from mild to resounding). Capitalism is obviously not a faultless system, and lively give-and-take discussion concerning its shortcomings is desirable. It is at least as important, however, to discuss the role of the private sector in creating a standard of living unrivaled in the history of civilization. How exportable is capitalism? How useful might it ultimately be for the nascent economies of Third World nations? CTIR prefers to give us discussions of a future which proposes limits on personal wealth (another possible future relating to "free enterprise" is a distorted caricature without any limits on personal or corporate behavior and no social "safety net"); other discussions urge consideration of uniform wages for all workers (regardless of job) and no private ownership of property.

The most transparent assault on market regulated economies is an exercise in which the teacher drops fistfuls of loose coins to the floor while prodding children to scramble after them. The students are then told to "redistribute" the money "more equitably" among themselves.

Repression Versus Revolution

There is even less balance to be found in CTIR's condemnation of apartheid. While no responsible person would seek to justify so repugnant an institution, it is interesting that CTIR devotes an entire book to the problem, but nowhere in their *Comparative World Issues* guide is there any mention of the fact that at least thirty other nations on the African continent embrace a racist ethos even more odious (if that were possible) than the one in Pretoria. Nor in any of their writings is there the faintest criticism of any Communist government.

"Right-wing dictators," however, seldom escape the wrath of globalists, and U.S. support for these regimes is predictably deplored by CTIR. Just as predictable is the absence of any examination of alternatives. How much more public policy insight might students gain by examining counterpoints raised in a recent issue of *National Review*:

1. U.S. liberals did everything in their power to bring down Chiang Kai-Shek, and in the process, gave the world Mao Tse-tung and thirty million corpses.

2. Our political-Left hated the corrupt Battista, so we got Castro's concentration camps and proxies for the instigation of Soviet proxy wars.

3. American left-wing opposition to the Shah played a major role in the advent of the Ayatollah.

4. Because the Thieu government was insufficiently pristine, U.S. anti-war activists gave communism to South Vietnam and half-a-million boat people to America.

5. U.S. liberals denounced Cambodia's Lon Nol as a CIA tool, so we got Pol Pot who exterminated two million of his own people.

6. Then, of course, there was leftist American pressure to topple despotic Somoza for the totalitarian Sandinistas.

7. Some also preferred the crippling Marxism of Salvador Allende to the present military government of Chile.

In every instance we lost an imperfect but non-imperialistic leader, to whose government we had access and on whose policies we had at least nominal influence. In their place we received Communist dictators from whom we were totally cut-off as they fomented "revolution without borders." Are any of their people better off? Students depending solely on CTIR materials for answers may never know.

Assaulting Family Integrity

One of the most disturbing aspects of the globalist curriculum, as outlined by CTIR, is the extent to which it invades the privacy of the traditional family to usurp prerogatives more properly left to parental discretion. Why would globalists encourage students to discuss issues and values on which they disagree with their parents? Why ask children to write essays discussing their mothers' and fathers' "faults"? Is it necessary to have students detail their feelings about their families and whether their homes are "happy places"? To what are their religious convictions and those of their families properly relevant in a classroom? How many parents would be enthusiastic about their children being asked to pass judgment on the correctness of the size of their families, or whether they should have fewer children than their grandparents and parents had? What business is it of teachers whether these children plan to marry, when they plan to do so, how large a family they intend to have and, if not, which "alternative lifestyle" they would prefer? Why do teachers need to know about the size and value of the family home, the monthly rent, and the number of cars the family owns?

Beyond Death Education

What is unquestionably the most bizarre section of any global education material, however, is the CTIR text on *death education*. To begin with, it surveys children to determine the extent to which they believe in "life after death" and how death is "talked about" in their families. The *World*

Citizen Curriculum contains a human evolutionary chart which suggests the absence of any afterlife. They are then told to chronicle a list of their darkest fears.

Intrusive questioning aside, it is at this point that the text becomes macabre. Children are told to project their own deaths by reading funeral notices, writing their own wills and obituaries, writing their own eulogies, designing their own gravestones, and reading actual suicide notes.

For unsurpassed morbidity, however, students can consider a lament that our culture does not encourage visits from the "spirits of the dead" (described as an "open and joyous experience" in contrast with American "uncomfortable" attitudes toward the dead). They are then taught to "create their own altar honoring the dead" (in a manner reminiscent of ancestor worship). Thereafter, they can make sacrifices of "alter offerings" on these icons. A later activity involves the construction and flying of kites bearing messages for the dead. Children are also asked to question which American death practices are "outmoded" and should be changed, such as burial with grave markers.

Consistent with the generally pacifistic tenor of globalist doctrine, students are advised to consider circumstances under which they would *not* be willing to die for their countries. Naturally, Vietnam is mentioned. Students are not, of course, asked to consider circumstances under which they *would* die for their country.

One possible explanation for this disturbing and forced confrontation with death can be found in the fact that these and other globalist materials contain the most pessimistic possible predictions for the future of planet Earth. Students are incessantly badgered with questions concerning the extent to which the human race is "headed for a disaster" and the "possibility of global death from atomic warfare or the collapse of the eco-system." It is one thing to have teenagers write a "eulogy for mankind"; that is rather remote and abstract. Students are more likely to be motivated to act in avoidance of "the disasters that could occur if present trends continue" and if the projected death is *their own*—up close and personal. That kind of mind-game makes the "peril" so much more real. And what can students do to avoid the coming apocalypse? The only alternative presented is the globalist vision of a new world order. Such a manipulative strategy squares nicely with the tactic of showing the same population control film three times to the same students, as is suggested by one lesson plan. The same can be said for the hyperbole contained in an environmental handout. It directs students to consider the possibility that defecating and urinating indiscriminately on the floor reflect "the direction of values in American society" as regards pollution. No less clever are the listings of comparative traits contributing to the "natural character" of societies in the eastern and western hemispheres. The Eastern column contains no negatives; the Western list has many.

The approach to spiritual matters is equally indirect, but many parents will no doubt find it problematic. In a "visualization exercise," children are placed in a trance-like state using transcendental meditative techniques (closed eyes, controlled breathing, deep relaxation, etc.) while a kind of cosmic tour guide mentally "advances them through the universe."

The concept of Biblical creation is rejected by omission, and none of the texts dealing with human rights (a spiritually related issue) makes any reference to prenatal justice and the rights of unborn children. The issue of abortion is handled in ways guaranteed to reinforce the assumption that killing unborn children is noncontroversial. *Teaching About Population Issues* by George Otero, Jr. (CTIR, 1983) refers to safe or legal abortions on pages 77, 81, 85, 103, 119 and 129 without mentioning that 98-99 percent of all abortions performed in America are convenience procedures done to end pregnancies that are an imposition but in no way imperil the mothers themselves. These readings further omit the fact that 95 percent of all abortions are performed between the tenth and eleventh weeks of pregnancy when babies are so fully developed that their brains are producing systematic brain wave activity (measurable with electroencephalogram); that their hearts have been beating strongly for weeks; that their lungs are "breathing" amniotic fluid in and out; that their livers are producing blood cells; that their kidneys are filtering blood; that their stomachs are secreting digestive enzymes; that they sleep and awaken in response to loud noises; and that they consistently turn away from bright light when shone in their faces via fiber optic illuminators inserted into their mother's wombs.

A full and fair examination of *all* relevant facts and arguments concerning this issue would enable students to approach the dilemma more objectively. They would at least have a clearer sense of the complexity and controversy which characterizes the problem.

Another interesting exercise has students reading the book *I Ching* and following its instructions on Chinese fortune-telling. Early American Christianity is described in unflattering terms that are only vaguely qualified at a later point. Again the problem is balance.

Students or Proselytes

In conclusion, most globalist curricular materials contain none of the crude anti-American polemics that characterized "New Left" denunciations of the 1960s. They have matured into a sophisticated series of Socratically delivered doctrinal bromides that no longer directly assail the core beliefs and assumptions of our American heritage. They seek, instead, to subtly ridicule our value system and suggest that we relinquish our economic and political preeminence in the interest of some shadowy "global justice."

This worldview is utopian, pacifist, and redistributionist. Although globalists decry doctrinaire absolutes, they paradoxically strive to replace conventional morality—based on Judeo-Christian principles—with an eclectic, mystical ethos of their own concoction. And they do so with a trace of ironic awareness.

When heat is applied to their curriculum, it distills into a hard left policy agenda. Their self-avowed objective is radical political change, and they intend to achieve it by turning students into activists.

While claiming commitment to "critical thinking," they repeatedly emotionalize policy decisions by attempting to evoke empathy, which encourages the kind of sympathetic hysteria that distorts judgment.

Why have so many school districts been so unquestioning in their acceptance of global education? One of the reasons may be that proponents of global education are often unwilling to volunteer disclosures concerning the more controversial aspects of their curriculum.

One effective form of deception is to simply infuse globalist concepts into existing courses on a teacher-by-teacher basis, thereby circumventing requirements for school board approval of new curricula.

Parents might be well advised to heed this caveat and pay careful attention to textbooks, lectures, and classroom activities.

Solutions

Must all global education be bad? Of course not. The problem is the virtual absence of *objective* curricular materials. With no alternatives to the bias of the political left, schools must ignore a serious academic need or serve it badly. The obvious solution is to break this left-wing monopoly by establishing a countervailing network of organizations producing intellectually honest materials.

[Former] U.S. Education Secretary William Bennett recently called America "the last best hope on earth." If it is to remain so, our children must first be taught why the most envied way of life in history is among the most fragile. The maintenance of representative democracy and a free enterprise economy requires enormous sacrifice. People don't sacrifice for things they don't appreciate, and they don't appreciate things they don't understand. But our children also need to learn that patriotic love of country and commitment to this nation's responsibility of leadership in a troubled world are in no way incompatible with an international consciousness that only a *well-balanced* program of global education can provide.

Our nation can no longer afford to debate the issue of whether to teach global education, but we must carefully and responsibly choose the global education programs we use.

Our inaction could mean nothing less than the future of this planet.

NOTES

Chapter 1: Turning the Hearts of the Young

1. Philip Vander Velde and Hyung-Chan Kim, eds., *Global Mandate: Pedagogy for Peace* (Bellingham, WA: Bellwether Press, 1985), 10.

Chapter 2: Masked Vision

1. Paul Johnson, *Intellectuals* (New York: Harper & Row, 1988), 340.

2. Lee Anderson, *School and Citizenship in a Global Age: An Exploration of the Meaning and Significance of Global Education* (Bloomington, Indiana: Social Studies Development Center, 1979).

3. Donald N. Morris, "Global Education in Elementary Schools: Implications for Curriculum and Instruction," *Social Education* (January 1977), 38.

4. Michael R. Simonson, "Global Awareness: A Curriculum Plan for World Study," *National Association for Secondary School Principals Bulletin* (October 1977), 75.

5. "U.S. Commission of Education Task Force on Global Education Report," *Developing Global Education Teaching Skills* (1979): 3. Distributed by the Office for Equity Education, the Office of the Superintendent of Public Instruction, Old Capitol Building, Olympia, WA 98504.

Chapter 3: What's Right About Global Education?

1. Lynda Carl Falkenstein, *Global Education: State of the Art Research Summary Report* (Portland, OR: Northwest Regional Educational Lab., 1983), 13. Distributed by the U.S. Dept. of Education, NIE, Education Resources Information Center, Washington, D.C. 20208).

Chapter 4: One World Culture: No More Western Civilization

1. Paul C. Vitz, "Religion and Traditional Values in Public School Text-books: An Empirical Study," Final Report: NIE-G84-0012, Project No. 2-0099; Equity in Values Education; U.S. Dept. of Education, 1985: 16.

2. Ibid., 32–33.

3. Ibid., 13.

4. Ibid., 29–30.

5. Ibid., 18.

6. Ibid., 71.

7. James M. Becker, ed., *Schooling for a Global Age* (New York: McGraw-Hill, 1979), 97.

8. Rick L. Hamblin, "A Transcultural Education Rationale," *Cultural Issues in Education* (Los Angeles: National Multilingual-Multicultural Materials Development Center, 1978): 2.

9. H. G. Vonk, *Phi Delta Kappa*, vol. 54, 514.

Chapter 5: Cultural Relativity: No More Absolutes

1. Falkenstein, *Global Education*, 14.

2. As quoted in Becker, *Schooling*, 212.

3. Wendell Bell, *Learning for Tomorrow: The Role of the Future in Education*, ed. Alvin Tofler (New York: Random House, 1974), 101. Quoting Fredrik L. Polak, *The Image of the Future*, vol. 1, (Oceania, N.Y., 1961), 36–37.

4. Gerald H. Paske, "The Failure of Indoctrination: A Response to Wynne," *Educational Leadership* (December/January 1986), 11.

5. William Kirk Kirkpatrick, *Psychological Seduction: The Failure of Modern Psychology* (Nashville: Thomas Nelson Pub., 1983), 53.

6. Nancy Stephan, et. al.; *Welcome to Earth: Culture Study Handbook for Elementary Schools*, 1985. A booklet distributed by Sunrise Elementary School, 2323 39th Ave. S.E., Puyallup, WA 98373, (206) 841-8744.

7. Erwin Lutzer, *The Necessity of Ethical Absolutes* (Grand Rapids, MI: Zondervan Pub. House, 1981), 20–21.

8. Allan Bloom, *The Closing of the American Mind* (New York: Simon and Schuster, 1987), 36.

9. Becker, *Schooling*, 45.

10. Harold G. Shane and June Grant Shane, "Educating the Youngest for Tomorrow," *Learning for Tomorrow: The Role of the Future in Education*, ed. Alvin Tofler (New York: Random House, 1974), 183.

11. "Seeking a Design for the Future: Immediate and Long-Range Plans of Louis Bruno, Washington State Superintendent of Public Instruction," 1968, 29.

12. "The Paramount Duty: Report of Washington State Temporary Committee on Educational Policies, Structures, and Managements," 1985, 43.

13. Falkenstein, *Global Education*, 15.

14. Bloom, *Closing*, 39.

Chapter 6: Political Resocialization: No More Patriotism

1. Ken Tye, Network News: "Bringing a global perspective to the classroom."

2. Falkenstein, *Global Education*, 23.

3. Richard Gross, et. al., *Social Studies for Our Times* (New York: John Wiley and Sons, 1978), 345.

4. Anna L. Rose Hawkes, *The World in Their Hands* (W. Lafayette, IN: Kappa Delta Pi, 1966), 25.

5. Richard MacLeod, "Internationalism: A Need in American Education," *The Clearinghouse*, vol. 49, no. 4 (December 1975): 178–179.

6. Lee Anderson, "An Examination of the Structure and Objectives of International Education," *Social Education*, no. 7 (November 1968): 647. As cited by Edith W. King, *The World: Context for Teaching in the Elementary School* (Dubuque, Iowa: Wm. C. Brown Pub., 1971), 156–157.

7. In the name of "learning activities" students are recruited into political activism. These activities also include writing letters to the President urging a reduction in nuclear arms and requiring students ot unthinkingly participate in "peace" rallies.

8. Falkenstein, *Global Education*, 24.

9. Ibid.

10. Bloom, *Closing*, 25–26.

11. Becker, *Schooling*, in forward by John Goodlad.

12. Becker, *Schooling*, 118. Donald N. Morris quoting Edith W. King from her, *Educating Young Children . . . Sociological Interpretations* (Dubuque, Iowa: Wm. C. Brown Co., 1973), 96.

13. Falkenstein, *Global Education*, 26.

14. Ibid.

15. Becker, *Schooling*.

16. As quoted by Bell, *Learning*, 141.

17. Becker, *Schooling.*

18. Ibid., 118.

19. Ibid., 100–101.

20. Anderson, as quoted by Becker, 28.

21. Becker, *Schooling,* 210.

22. Irving H. Buchen, *Learning for Tomorrow: The Role of the Future in Education,* ed. Alvin Tofler (New York: Random House, 1974).

Chapter 7: The New Age Agenda

1. Dick Sutphen, "Infiltrating the New Age into Society," *What Is,* Vol. 1, No. 1.

2. Robert Muller, *New Genesis: Shaping A Global Spirituality* (Garden City, N.Y.: Image Books, Doubleday and Co., Inc., 1984), 8.

3. Ibid., 54.

4. Ibid., 41, 120–121, 126.

5. Ibid., 125, 49.

6. Ibid., 165–166.

7. Ibid., 43–44.

8. Susan Hooper, "Educator Proposes a Global 'Core Curriculum,'" *Education Week* (November 27, 1985): 8.

9. Ibid.

10. Muller, *New Genesis,* 145.

11. Hooper, "Educator," 8.

12. Muller, *New Genesis,* 150.

13. Dane Rudhyar, *Occult Preparations for a New Age* (Wheaton, IL: The Theosophical Publishing House, 1975), 69.

14. Muller, *New Genesis,* 152.

15. Hooper, "Educator," 8.

16. Muller, *New Genesis,* 152.

17. Hooper, "Educator," 8.

18. Muller, *New Genesis,* 152.

19. Ibid., 153.

20. Ibid., 155.

21. Ibid., 94.

22. Ibid., 164.

23. Ibid., 191.

24. For more information on the World University Development Association, write to: P.O. Box 33739 Station D, Vancouver, B.C. V6J 4L6 Canada.

25. *The World Core Curriculum in the Robert Muller School*, prepared by The School of Ageless Wisdom, 6005 Royal Oak Dr., Arlington, TX 76016, (817) 654-1018.

26. Alice A. Bailey, *Initiation: Human and Solar* (Albany, NY: Lucis Trust, Fort Orange Press, Inc., 1951), 57.

27. Eileen Lynch, et al., *Evaluation Report of THE ROBERT MULLER SCHOOL for the SOUTHERN ASSOCIATION OF COLLEGES AND SCHOOLS* (October 1984) 2, 5, 6, 14, 22.

Chapter 8: New Agers in the Public Schools

1. Muller, *New Genesis*, 132.

2. Dick Sutphen, *What Is*, vol. 1, no. 1 (Reincarnationalists, Box 3009, Agoura Hills, CA 91301, 1986), 27.

3. Marilyn Ferguson, *The Aquarian Conspiracy: Personal and Social Transformation in the 1980s* (Los Angeles: J. P. Tarcher, Inc., 1980), 280–281.

4. Ibid., 282.

5. Ibid., 371.

6. Ibid., 372.

7. Ibid.

8. Ibid., 288.

9. Ibid., 295.

10. Ibid., 288.

11. Gay Hendricks and Thomas B. Roberts, *The Second Centering Book: More Awareness Activities for Children, Parents, and Teachers* (Englewood Cliffs, NJ: Prentice-Hall, Inc., 1977).

12. Ibid., 224.

13. Jack Canfield, "Education in the New Age," *New Age*, vol. 3, no. 9 (February 1978): 36.

14. Rudhyar, *Occult Preparation*, 262.

15. D. Scott Rogo, *Leaving the Body: A Complete Guide to Astral Projection* (Englewood Cliffs, NJ: Prentice Hall, Inc., 1983), 116.

16. Shakti Gawain, *Creative Visualization* (New York: Bantam Books, 1982), 120.

17. Beverly Galyean, *Language from Within* (Longbeach, CA: , 1976), 91. As told by Dave Hunt in *Peace, Prosperity, and the Coming Holocaust* (Eugene, OR: Harvest House Pub., 1983), 78.

18. Frances Adeney, "Educators Look East," *SCP Journal*, vol. 5, no. 1 (Winter 1981–1982): 29.

19. Melita Denning and Osborne Phillips, *The Llewellyn Practical Guide to Creative Visualization: For the Fulfillment of Your Desires* (St. Paul, MN: Llewellyn Pub., 1985), 31.

20. Ibid., 65.

21. As quoted by Adeney, "Educators Look East," 29.

22. Gawain, *Creative*, 71.

23. As quoted by Adeney, "Educators Look East," 30.

24. Ruth Montgomery, *Strangers Among Us* (New York: Fawcett Crest, 1979), 109.

25. Elmer and Alyce Green, *Beyond Biofeedback* (New York: 1979), 56.

26. Ferguson, *Aquarian Conspiracy*, 314.

Chapter 9: Hypnotizing Children into the Occult

1. The quotes from *Mission S.O.A.R.* come from a pilot curriculum used in the Los Angeles, California, public schools. Because the program is being field tested and not yet in final form, indicating specific page numbers for locating lessons will prove useless. Complete documentation can be obtained by written request from Dr. Lulu Lopez, Office of Instruction, L.A.U.S.D., Room A-301, 450 N. Grand, Los Angeles, CA 90012. Due to public pressure this program may change.

2. William W. Hewitt, *Beyond Hypnosis: A Program for Developing Your Psychic and Healing Power* (St. Paul, MN: Llewellyn Publication, 1990), 83.

3. Ibid., 84.

4. Ibid., 144.

5. Ibid., 152, 154.

6. Ibid., 203.

7. Ibid., 85.

8. Ibid., 177.

9. Ferguson, *Aquarian Conspiracy*, 79–80.

10. Ibid., 296.

11. Ibid., 315.

12. Ibid., 168–169.

13. Montgomery, *Strangers Among Us*, 151.

14. Ibid., 70–71.

15. Rudhyar, *Occult Preparations*, 149.

16. Ferguson, *Aquarian Conspiracy*, 108–109.

17. Ibid., 113.

18. Ibid.

19. For more information on Windstar, write to New Awareness Consultants at P.O. Box 5181, Golden, CO 80401. Ask for their book, *Grave New World*.

Chapter 10: The Call for One World Government

1. Johnson, *Intellectual*, 342.

2. Vander Velde, *Global Mandate*, 354.

3. Ibid., 26.

4. Fritjof Capra, *The Turning Point* (New York: Bantam Books, 1982), 78.

5. Ibid., 87.

6. Ibid., 35.

7. Ibid., 416.

8. Ibid., 412.

9. Vander Velde, *Global Mandate*, 17.

10. Capra, *Turning Point*, 33.

11. Vander Velde, *Global Mandate*, 25.

12. Ibid., 26.

13. Ibid., 103.

14. Ibid., 351.

15. Ibid., 10.

16. Ibid., 21.

17. Ibid., 22.

18. Ibid., 35.

19. Ibid., 352–353.

20. Ibid., 6.

21. Ibid., 37.

22. Ibid., 23.

23. Ibid., 31.

24. Ibid., 32.

25. Capra, *Turning Point*, 396.

SELECTED BIBLIOGRAPHY

Becker, James, ed. *Schooling for a Global Age.* New York: Mc-Graw-Hill, 1979.

Developing Global Education Teaching Skills: A compendium of excerpts from materials written by educators advocating global education in the American school system; distributed by the Office of Equity Education, Office of Superintendent of Public Instruction, Old Capitol Building, Olympia, Washington 98504.

Ferguson, Marilyn. *The Aquarian Conspiracy: Personal and Social Transformation in the 1980s.* Los Angeles: J. P. Tarcher, Inc., 1980.

Global Education: State of the Art Research Summary Report. Northwest Regional Educational Lab.; distributed by the U.S. Dept. of Education, NIE, Education Resources Information Center, Washington, D.C. 20208.

Muller, Robert. *The New Genesis: Shaping a Global Spirituality.* Garden City, New York: Image Books, a Division of Doubleday and Co., Inc., 1984.

Vander Velde, Philip, and Hyung-chan Kim, eds. *Global Mandate: Pedagogy for Peace.* Western Washington University, Bellingham, WA: Bellwether Press, 1985. Write to the Center for Global Peace Education, School of Education, Western Washington University, Bellingham, WA 98225.

INDEX

ABOUT THE AUTHOR

E ric Buehrer is the executive vice president of the National Association of Christian Educators/Citizens for Excellence in Education. Formerly a high school history teacher in an inner-city school, Mr. Buehrer now travels widely speaking to parents, teachers, and concerned citizens regarding public school issues affecting the Christian family.

His current work involves organizing and training Christian parents to impact the public schools with a Christian perspective. He authored and conducts *Charting Your Family's Course*, family education seminars, across America. Mr. Buehrer is a highly sought-after speaker for seminars, banquets, radio, and television.

He and his wife, Kim, reside in southern California.

If you find this book helpful, please write: National Association of Christian Educators/Citizens for Excellence in Education, P. O. Box 3200, Costa Mesa, CA 92628.

The typeface for the text of this book is *Palatino*. This type—best known as a contemporary *italic* typeface—was a post-World War II design crafted by the talented young German calligrapher Hermann Zapf. For inspiration, Zapf drew upon the writing legacy of a group of Italian Renaissance writing masters, in which the typeface's namesake Giovanni Battista Palatino was numbered. Giovanni Palatino's *Libro nuovo d'imparare a scrivera* was published in Rome in 1540 and became one of the most used, wide-ranging writing manuals of the sixteenth century. Zapf was an apt student of the European Masters, and contemporary *Palatino* is one of his contributions to modern typography.

Substantive Editing:
Michael S. Hyatt

Copy Editing:
Susan Kirby

Cover Design:
Steve Diggs & Friends
Nashville, Tennessee

Page Composition:
Xerox Ventura Publisher
Printware 720 IQ Laser Printer

Printing and Binding:
Maple-Vail Book Manufacturing Group
York, Pennsylvania

Cover Printing:
Weber Graphics
Chicago, Illinois

Protect Your Public School Child

How to Start a Public School Awareness Committee in Your Church

A Public School Awareness (PSA) committee is a dynamic way to keep your entire church aware of what is happening in your local schools. It will help parents, grandparents, and other concerned citizens protect children from harmful public school programs.

Because of the guidance of the PSA kit, the PSA committee is easy to start and practical to use. This kit contains audio cassette tapes, and a three-ring bound notebook with all the material you will need for success. Parent Action Guides included in the kit show exactly how to participate in petition drives, activate letter writing campaigns, initiate phone calling of public officials, and speak at school board meetings. Your PSA kit also gives you access to other active parent groups who have already worked on many of the issues you will be facing. By accessing that network you can receive invaluable advice and research from experienced parents involved in public schools.

To receive a brochure on ordering a PSA kit for your church, fill out this coupon and return it to the address below. Just for sending in the coupon, you will receive a free subscription to *Education Newsline*—news and commentary on public school issues affecting the Christian family.

Name: _____

Address: _____

Phone: (_____) _____

Citizens for Excellence in Education
Box 3200
Costa Mesa, CA 92628